THE MAMMALS OF ARUNACHAL PRADESH

THE MAMMALS OF ARUNACHAL PRADESH

Written & Illustrated
by
Anwaruddin Choudhury

Regency Publications
New Delhi

The designations of geographical entities in this publication and the presentation of the material, do not imply expression of any opinion whatsoever concerning the legal status on any country, territory, or area, or of its authorities, or concerning the delimitation of its frontiers or boundaries.

ISBN 81-87498-80-3

Published by Regency Publications, 20/36-G, Old Market, West Patel Nagar, New Delhi 110 008 and printed at Radiant Printers, New Delhi 110 008. Phone: 2571 2539 • Telefax: 2578 3571 • Email: regency@satyam.net.in • www.regency-books.com.

PREFACE

This is the firstever checklist and systematic review of the mammals of Arunachal Pradesh, a state having the highest mammalian diversity in India. However, this is not the first in the region. *The checklist of the mammals of Assam* (1994, revised second edition in 1997) was the first attempt to systematically document the mammals in north-eastern India. While many species are similar to both the states, there are high elevation forms, which are confined to Arunachal Pradesh only. It was surmised that perhaps Assam has the highest mammalian diversity in India with 189 ± species (Choudhury, 1997e) but this checklist has already crossed 200 mark (206 species) with another 38 species likely to occur or are recorded in adjacent areas.

A checklist supported by accurate illustrations is useful both for casual nature-enthusiast as well as serious students of zoology and allied subjects. This work is intended to be like that. The present work is based upon both primary and secondary sources. The more than a decade-long field work (direct sightings in the wild, records of wild-caught animals held as captives, etc) in Arunachal Pradesh and examination of preserved specimens by me provided for the main primary data while published documents, such as books, journals, popular articles, research reports, etc., alongwith unpublished materials, reports by experienced hunters, Forest officials and other observers contributed for the secondary data.

Museum specimens have been examined at different collections, notably at the National Museum of Natural History (Smithsonians, Washington), American Museum of Natural History (New York), Field Museum of Natural History (Chicago), Museum of Vertebrate Zoology (University of California, Berkeley), Wildlife Conservation Society (New York), Zoological Survey of India (Kolkata [Calcutta] and Shillong), Natural History Museum (Darjeeling), Itanagar Museum, Forest department's Museum (Shillong and Guwahati), collections at the museums of Project Tiger at Miao (near Namdapha National Park), and many private collections spread across Arunachal Pradesh, especially in the tribal villages.

However, works on the bats and small mammals such as the rodents continued to be very scanty and the text in this checklist also indicates the same. The checklist is followed by an exhaustive bibliography on the mammals, especially pertaining to the region and includes almost all the original descriptions included or referred to in the text. Many of these works have also been consulted while preparing this book.

In most cases, the conservation status of different species according to CITES, IUCN (2002) and the Indian Wild Life (Protection) Act 1972 have been given. Explanatory notes on taxonomic status, wherever there is confusion, have been given in 'remarks' section accompanying the species notes.

The species have been serially numbered while the subspecies have been given the same serial with suffix a,b, etc. The serial numbers in *The checklist of the mammals of Assam* (1997e) are given in parenthesis for convenience of reference. It may be mentioned here that many of the subspecific classification are not concrete and need detailed review.

It is hoped that this book will be of use to a broad audience and also help in planning for conservation in this biodiversity-rich area.

December 5, 2002

ANWARUDDIN CHOUDHURY
Near Gate No.1 of Nehru Stadium,
7, Islampur Road, Guwahati 781 007
(Assam) India
email: badru1@sancharnet.in

ACKNOWLEDGEMENTS

A large number of people have extended help in the work and I thank them all. However, the following deserve mention: S.N. Kalita, CCF; late R.P. Neog, Yogesh, both former Field Directors of Namdapha; A. Sen, C. Reddy, M.M.S. Negi, Pratap Singh, M.K. Palit, C. Loma, R. Horo, R.K. Das, all DFOs; Pankaj Sharma, P. Das, Dewri, A.K. Singh, S.K. Shome, all Range Officers, A.K. Ghose and B.C. Dey, Foresters, and T. Hazarika, Forest Guard, Ramalingam, Moniram Gogoi, Dorji Raptan, Tenzing Phiyan, Rajesh Pachung (all ex-sanctuary watchers), Srimanta Tamuli, Ratnesh Rai, Pemba Tamang, Kancha Tamang, Amit Glow and other staff based at Anchalghat, Bogoli, Bomjir, Dambuk, Deban, Dirang, Dirgha, Khari, Mayodia, Miao, Pasighat, Ramalingam, Roing, Santipur, Seijosa, Sessa, Sundarview, Tawang, Tipi, Wakro, and Ziro; Ms Emily Chowdhary, former Development Commissioner for Hill Areas, Assam; Nur Husain, Dilip Handique, late Sakul Boro, Babul Debnath, Faizul Ali, Hakeem Choudhury, Bisoy Boro, Moniram Boro (last seven are all drivers); Ratul Talukdar and Faruq of The Rhino Foundation; Nitu Phukan of Eco-camp, Leto Mili of Dambuk; wife of B.C. Hazarika, Forest Guard, Ramalingam; Bir Bahadur Gurung, S. Majumder (of GREF), P. Chuppa, Munu Kashyap, Dr. P. Dewri of Tawang, Dr Tacho of Sangti, Sonu Sonar of Dirang IB, Lobsan Chander, Darge Tsering, Kuppa, Dorji Nima, Pema Yeshi, Lama Pema, R. Norbu, Gambo Tsering, Abraham, S.K. Shome, S. Kalita of Sangti, Namge Dorji, Pema Yaoundi, Gajen Tamang, Lei Kandu Thungon, late Ledo Thungon, K.N. Thungon, B.B. Bhatt, D. Tamuk, Sitẹm Borang, Mamata Riba, Tsering Naksong, Tater Hiba, Tape Mosing, Bikul Goswami; Samar Singh, A.R.K. Shastry, and A.K. Goswami of WWF-India; and Bablu Dey and Subhash Chanda of Green Heart, Kokrajhar.

Lastly, I would like to make a mention of my family members who always stood by me giving all kinds of support.

CONTENTS

Preface v
Acknowledgements vii

Introduction 1
Systematic List 9
Order Pholidota: Pangolins 9
Order Insectivora: Insectivores 10
Order Scandentia: Tree-shrews 15
Order Chiroptera: Bats 16
Order Primates: Primates 31
Order Carnivora: Carnivores 41
Order Cetacea: Whales, Dolphins and Porpoises 62
Order Proboscidea: Elephants 63
Order Perissodactyla: Odd-toed ungulates 65
Order Artiodactyla: Even-toed ungulates 67
Order Rodentia: Rodents 80
Order Lagomorpha: Hares, Rabbits and Pikas 97

Appendix 1. Species not Recorded but Occur in the Adjoining Areas 101
Appendix 2. Protected Areas in Arunachal Pradesh (Area in Km^2) 103
Appendix 3. Main Reserved Forests (Area in Km^2) 104
Bibliography 107
Index 133

INTRODUCTION

The state of Arunachal Pradesh (26°40′–29°27′ N, 91°35′–97°24′ E) covers an area of 83,700 km^2, and forms part of a rich biogeographic unit that represents one of the biodiversity 'Hotspots' (Myers, 1988, 1991). It also forms part of the Eastern Himalaya Endemic Bird Area (Collar *et al.*, 1994). The state is mostly hilly and mountainous being part of the Eastern Himalaya. The mountains towards east of the Siang River are known as Mishmi Hills. Farther eastern and south-eastern areas are dominated by the Dapha Bum and Patkai Ranges. Small areas of flat plain occur along the larger rivers such as the Siang, Dibang and the Lohit. The higher areas, especially the peaks of the Great Himalaya remain snow-capped throughout the year.

Arunachal Pradesh has 15 districts, namely, Tawang, W. Kameng, E. Kameng, Upper Subansiri, Lower Subansiri, Papum Pare, Upper Siang, W. Siang, E. Siang, Dibang Valley, Lohit, Changlang and Tirap (two have been added recently—Kurung Kamei and Upper Dibang Valley). The present state came into existence in 1987. Originally this tract was administered by the Governor of Assam and was divided into three large divisions, Balipara Frontier Tract (present Tawang, W. Kameng, E. Kameng, Upper Subansiri, Lower Subansiri and Papum Pare districts), Sadiya Frontier Tract (present Upper Siang, W. Siang, E. Siang, Dibang Valley and Lohit Districts) and Tirap Frontier Tract (present Changlang and Tirap Districts). Till 1972, it was known as NEFA (North-East Frontier Agency). In 1972 it was renamed as Arunachal Pradesh and was administered as a union territory till 1987.

Physiographically, the major parts of Arunachal Pradesh are hilly and mountainous. The Great Himalaya covers part of Tawang, W. Kameng, E. Kameng, Upper Subansiri, Lower Subansiri, W. Siang and Upper Siang districts. Lesser Himalayas cover parts of W. Kameng, E. Kameng, Upper Subansiri, Lower Subansiri, Papum Pare, W. Siang and E. Siang districts. The Mishmi Hills cover parts of E. Siang, Dibang Valley and Lohit districts. The Dapha Bum Range, often referred to as part of Mishmi Hills cover parts of

Lohit and Changlang districts while Patkai Range covers Tirap and Changlang districts. The highest peak is Kangto, 7090 m (23,260 ft). Other high peaks include Nyegi Kangtsang, 7047 m (23,120 ft.), Chomo, 6937 m (22,760 ft.) and Gorichen, 6538 m (21,450 ft.), all in the Great Himalaya.

The climate of Arunachal Pradesh (except for the Great Himalaya and higher areas of Lesser Himalaya, which may be termed as 'mountain type') is tropical 'monsoon' type with a hot wet summer and a cool dry winter. Winter rains are also not uncommon. Annual rainfall of the state varies from less than 1500 mm to more than 4000 mm. The south-facing slopes of the Himalaya and Mishmi Hills, and the north-facing slopes of the Patkai Range receive very heavy rainfall. At places such as Dambuk and Khonsa, there are records of more than 10,000 mm in a year. The temperature generally ranges from –0° C in winter (minimum) to 35° C in summer (maximum). The main features of mountain climate are sharp contrast between sun and shade temperature, high diurnal range of temperature, inversion of temperature and variability of rainfall depending upon exposure and elevation (Singh, 1976). Breathing is difficult above 3050 m due to low percentage of oxygen.

Arunachal Pradesh has widely differing habitats. Tropical wet evergreen forests occur mainly in the eastern areas covering parts of Tirap, Changlang, Lohit and Dibang Valley districts. A linear strip of such forest occurs all along the Lesser Himalayan ranges from W. Kameng to E. Siang districts. Some important tree species found in such forests are the Hollong *Dipterocarpus macrocarpus* (confined to the eastern areas, south of the Lohit R.), Sia-nahor *Kayea assamica* (confined to the lower hills of Papum Pare, Lower Subansiri and West Siang districts), Mekai *Shorea assamica*, Nahor *Mesua ferrea*, Hollock *Terminalia myriocarpa*, Khokan *Duabanga sonneratioides* and Cham-kothal *Artocarpus chaplasha*. Altitudinally, such type of forest occurs from plains (*c*. 100 m) to 900 m.

Tropical semi-evergreen forests occur along the *bhabar* tract in the *duars*, all along from W. Kameng to E. Siang districts. In the south bank region, such forests are found wherever human interference was there. Besides the main evergreen species mentioned earlier, a large number of deciduous trees are also found, these include Bhelu *Tetrameles nudiflora*, Udal *Sterculia villosa* and Simul or Silk cotton *Bombax ceiba*. This type of forest occurs from plains to up to 600 m.

The higher altitudes of the Himalaya, Mishmi Hills and Patkai Range have subtropical forest having both broadleaf as well as

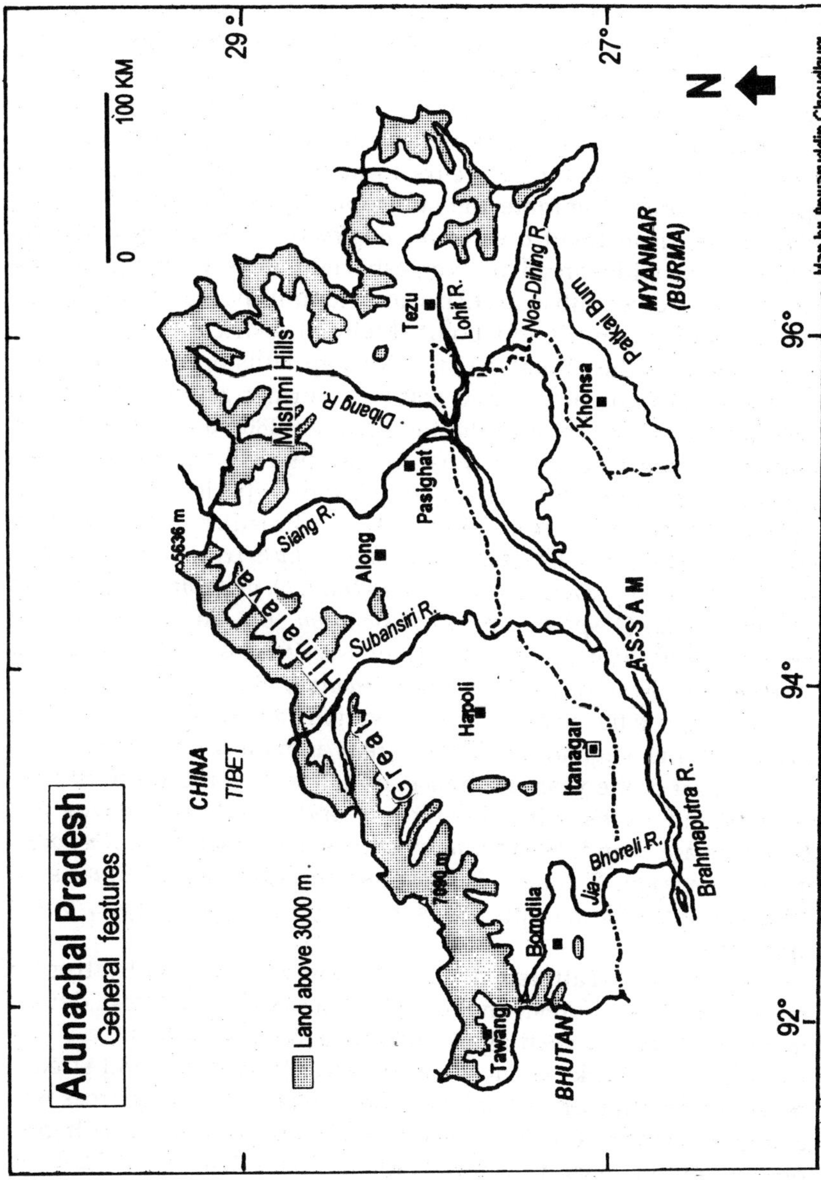
Arunachal Pradesh
General features
Land above 3000 m
0
100 KM
N
CHINA
TIBET
BHUTAN
MYANMAR
(BURMA)
ASSAM
Great Himalaya
Mishmi Hills
Patkai Bum
5636 m
7090 m
Tawang
Bomdila
Itanagar
Hapoli
Along
Pasighat
Tezu
Khonsa
Jia-Bhoreli R.
Brahmaputra R.
Subansiri R.
Siang R.
Dibang R.
Lohit R.
Noa-Dihing R.
29°
27°
92°
94°
96°
Map by Anwaruddin Choudhury

conifers. While the broadleaf forest generally occurs between 800 and 1900 m elevation, the conifers, usually between 1000 and 1800 m, especially in areas receiving less amount of rainfall. Various species of oaks dominate the broadleaf species. Some major species found in such forest type are *Acer oblongum, Castanopsis armata, C. hystrix, C. lidica, Manglietia insignis, Michelia oblonga, Ostodes paniculata, Quercus fenestrata, Q. griffithii, Q. lamellosa, Q. semiserrata, Q. spicata, Schima khasiana, S. wallichii* and *Ulnus lancifolium.* Except Tirap, such type of forest occurs in all the other districts. Three species of pines dominate the subtropical pine forests. These are *Pinus merkusii* in Lohit dist, *P. roxburghii* in W. Kameng dist, and *P. wallichiana* widespread all over, especially in W. Kameng (Dirang and Rupa), Lower Subansiri (Ziro and Hapoli), W. Siang (Mechuka), Dibang Valley (Anini) and Lohit (Melinja) districts.

Farther up the Himalaya, and Mishmi Hills occur the temperate forest, both broadleaf and conifers. Former generally between 1800 and 2800 m while the latter between 2800 and 3500 m. The temperate forest occurs in most of the districts except for Tirap, Papum Pare and bulk of Changlang. Various species of oaks, magnolias and rhododendrons dominate the broadleaf species, especially *Acer oblongum, Castanopsis armata, C. hystrix, C. lidica, Michelia oblonga, Populus gamblei, Quercus fenestrata, Q. griffithii, Q. lamellosa, Q. semiserrata, Q. spicata* and *Rhododendron* spp. The main conifers are *Pinus wallichiana, Tsuga* spp., *Cupressues torulosa, Abies spectabilis, A. delavayi, Taxus baccata, Juniperus recurva,* etc.

Between 4000 and 5500 m elevation, above the timber line, occurs alpine vegetation. These areas remain snow covered for greater part of the year and hence, no tall trees could grow. Shrubs, bushes and herbs with deep roots and cushioned leaves and branches are found. Some noteworthy species found are *Rhododendron anthopogon, R. nivale, R. thomsonii, Arenaria* spp., *Festuca* spp., *Rhodiola* spp., *Rheum* spp., *Saussaurea* spp., *Saxifraga* spp., *Sedum* spp., etc.

Small areas scattered here and there are covered by tropical moist deciduous forest, mainly plantations by the forest department with species such as the teak tree *Tectona grandis.*

Along the banks of most of the larger hilly rivers and streams occur the riverine or riparian fringing forest. A few large trees with a large number of shrubs, both evergreen and deciduous with grass on the ground characterise this type of forest. The Sissoo *Dalbergia sissoo* and Khair *Acacia catechu* are the characteristic trees of such type. On the *chars* and *chapories* (sandy islets and tracts) of the

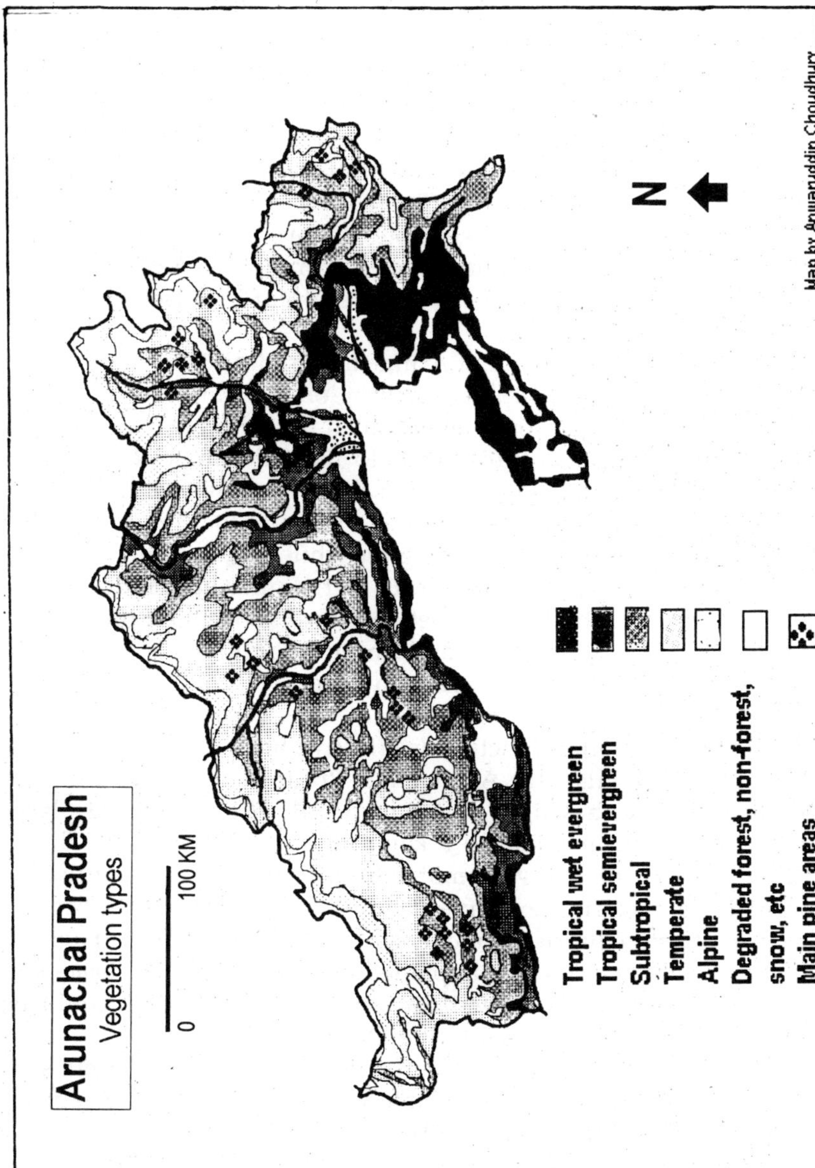
Arunachal Pradesh
Vegetation types
0
100 KM
N
Tropical wet evergreen
Tropical semievergreen
Subtropical
Temperate
Alpine
Degraded forest, non-forest, snow, etc
Main pine areas
Map by Anwaruddin Choudhury

Siang, Dibang, Lohit and their larger tributaries, pine-like Jhau *Tamarix dioica* shrub occurs abundantly.

In the floodplain zone of the Siang, Dibang, Lohit and the Noa-Dihing occurs wet savanna grassland with tall elephant-grass, reeds and *Alpinia allughas* herbs. Some such grassland pockets are found in D'Ering Memorial W.S., Dibang RF, tract between the Siang and the Sesseri rivers, and along the Lohit R. The main species of grasses found in such grasslands are Khagori *Phragmites karka*, Nal *Arundo donax*, *Neyraudia reynaudiana*, Ekra *Erianthus ravannae*, Ulu kher *Imperata cylindrica* and Thatch *Saccharum spontaneum*, *S. arundinaceum*, etc. Some trees like Bogori *Zizyphus* spp, Koroi *Albizzia procera* and Simul or Silk cotton are found scattered in the grasslands. In the higher areas, grassses occur profusely as undergrowth in pine forests.

Broadly speaking, bulk of Arunachal Pradesh forms part of the Himalayan (zoogeographic) Subregion within the Oriental Zoogeographic Region (now often called the Indomalayan Region). This subregion is also transitional to the Palaearctic Region as a number of Palaearctic taxa occur in the area. However, if we look into microlevel details, then the eastern Arunachal Pradesh seems to be part of Indochinese Subregion while the Indian Subregion lies towards extreme south-west. In fact, Arunachal Pradesh is located in the transitional zone between two zoogeographic regions (Oriental and Palaearctic), and three subregions (Himalayan, Indochinese and Indian) where many species have met with recessions on all sides.

Large rivers often function as effective barriers in the distribution of mammals. In Arunachal Pradesh and Assam, the Brahmaputra R., having a minimum width of *c.* 1.5 km (at places more than 5 km) has played a key role in determining the distribution pattern of many mammalian species. The distribution of primates is a glaring example (Choudhury, 1989f). The river has been an effective barrier to movement and dispersal of the Hoolock gibbon *Hylobates hoolock*, Stumptailed macaque *Macaca arctoides* and Pigtailed macaque *M. nemestrina*. Similarly, no langurs could be found between the Siang and the Dibang rivers.

There is little published information on the mammals of Arunachal Pradesh. Some available works are Borang & Thapliyal (1993), Chakraborty & Sen (1991), Chatterjee (1989), Chatterjee & Chandiramani (1986), Choudhury (1988a, 1991c, 1992a, 1994b, 1995a,d, 1996g,h, 1997f,g,h, 1998a, 1998b, 1999a,b,c,d), Ghosh (1987), Katti *et al.*, (1990), Saha (1984, 1985), Singh (1991), Singh *et al.*,

Plates

Elephants *Elephas maximus*

A Hoolock gibbon male
Hylobates hoolock

Bharal or Blue Sheep horn

Takin *Budorcas taxicolor*

Assamese macaque *Macaca assamensis*

Forrest's Pika *Ochotona forresti*

(1994, 1995, 1996), Thomas (1914a,b), and Vanak & Goyal (1996). General information on different species of mammals found in Arunachal Pradesh (often referred to as Assam or NEFA) are found in some synoptic works, notably those of Agrawal (1975), Blanford (1888, 1891), Blyth (1863), Choudhury (1986b, 1987a, 1989f, 1997a, 1997e, 2000), Corbett & Hill (1992), Ellerman & Morrison-Scott (1951), Gee (1964), McClelland (1839), Pocock (1939, 1941), and Prater (1948).

The systematics and nomenclature, including sequence of orders and families in this work largely follow Corbet & Hill (1992). Ellerman & Morrison-Scott (1951) and Wilson & Reeder (1993) were also taken into account wherever necessary. Departures from Corbet & Hill (1992) are relatively few, mostly at subspecies level with some at genus level. Attempt have been made to justify all such deviations with explanations given in 'Remarks' section that has accompanied most of the species accounts.

Altogether 241 forms including species and subspecies have been included in this edition. The total number of species listed here is 206, which includes two recently extinct forms. However, occurrence of at least 10 species is not beyond doubt. Another 38 species are suspected to occur. Presence of such a diverse mammalian species in a relatively small area is quite significant (*c.* 65% of the total mammalian species found in india). This is perhaps the highest diversity of mammals for any of the Indian states.

In the text, the *duars* have been referred to on a number of occasions. The alluvial, often undulating and also marshy (at places) strip of land stretching along the southern edge of the Himalaya, composed of grassland (*terai*) and forest (*bhabar*), now interspersed with cultivation and tea plantation, from Jalpaiguri dist of West Bengal to about Sonitpur dist of Assam is called the *Duars*. There is hardly any *terai* grassland inside Arunachal Pradesh but *bhabar* tract is conspicuous. The districts (part) covered inside Arunachal Pradesh are West and East Kameng, and Papum Pare. Southern part of Pakhui W.S. and Papum RF are typical examples of *bhabar* tract.

Conservation problems. Deforestation through commercial felling and *jhum* cultivation, and poaching for items of international trade such as musk, ivory, bear biles, tiger-bone and skins of various species, and of course for the pot are the main conservation issues. Demand for firewood in the high altitude areas in winter for room-heating, and road construction are also responsible for degradation of habitat. Between 1993 and 1995 (assessment years), Arunachal Pradesh has lost 334 km² of dense forest (*Source*: State of Forest Report, 1995).

The following abbreviations have been used in the text:

A	= Assamese.
AUC	= Reference to unpublished materials of author.
BS	= Bird Sanctuary.
CITES	= Convention on International Trade in Endangered Species.
Dist.	= District.
E	= East, eastern.
IUCN	= World Conservation Union (formerly International Union for Conservation of Nature & Natural Resources); CR: Critically endangered; EN: Endangered; VU: Vulnerable; LR: Lower risk; CD: Conservation dependent; NT: Near threatened; LC: Least concerned; DD: Data deficient.
WPA	= Wild Life (Protection) Act.
N	= North, northern.
NE	= North-east, north-eastern.
NP	= National Park.
NW	= North-west, north-western.
pc	= Personal communication.
R	= River.
RF	= Reserve Forest.
S	= South, southern.
SE	= South-east, south-eastern.
Sp., sp.	= Species (plural: spp.).
Ssp, ssp.	= Subspecies.
Syn	= Synonym.
SW	= South-west, south-western.
W	= West, western.
WS	= Wildlife Sanctuary.

SYSTEMATIC LIST

Order PHOLIDOTA

Pangolins

The order Pholidota comprises the Pangolins or Scaly ant-eaters of the Old World. The sloths and armadillos (Order Xenarthra) of the Neotropical Region are their close relatives. These toothless animals feed exclusively on ants and termites with the help of their long protrusible and glutinous tongue. They have an armour of overlapping scales, which is unique. It is represented by one family and one species in Arunachal Pradesh.

Family MANIDAE

Pangolins

(1) **1. *Manis pentadactyla*** Chinese pangolin
M. pentadactyla Linnaeus, 1758: 36. TYPE-LOCALITY: Taiwan.

Local Names. *Bonrou* (A), *Hochik* (Adi), *Hahbit* (Wancho).

Distribution & Status. Common in the forests and grasslands all over. Affects both plains and hills. Found in almost all the protected areas.

Subspecies. 1a *M. p. auritus*
M. auritus Hodgson, 1836: 234. TYPE-LOCALITY: Lower and central Nepal.

Chinese pangolin

Remarks. Only one subspecies occurs within Indian limits. However, subspecific classification needs a review. The pangolins in Arunachal Pradesh are often misidentified as Indian species *M. crassicaudata* (Chatterjee, 1989; Singh *et al.*, 1994). One of the main distinguishing features is the presence of 15–18 rows of scales in *M. pentadactyla* against 11–13 in *M. crassicaudata*.
CITES: Appendix II; IUCN: LR (nt); WPA: Schedule I.

Order INSECTIVORA

Insectivores

Hedgehogs, moles, shrews or ground shrews, etc., are classified as Insectivora, the insect-eating mammals. They are comparatively small animals. Most are also nocturnal. All of them have a characteristic, long and pointed snout projecting far beyond the lower jaw. The moles and ground shrews live underground while the tree-shrews (now excluded) are arboreal. Of some nine different families of recognised Insectivora, two occur in Arunachal Pradesh. They are Talpidae (moles), and Soricidae (shrews or ground shrews). The tree-shrews (family Tupaiidae) which have been included in the past, are here placed in a separate order Scandentia. The classification of the Insectivora and the uncertainty relating to the taxonomic status of the tree-shrews have been reviewed by Gill (1875), Cabrera (1925), Van Valen (1967), Campbell (1974), Gureev (1979) and Butler (1988).

Family TALPIDAE

Moles

Subfamily TALPINAE

(3) **2. *Talpa micrura*** Himalayan, or Indian short-tailed mole
T. micrura Hodgson, 1841b: 221. TYPE-LOCALITY: Nepal.

Local Names. *Ûk-muk, Ûtonua* (A), *Kurt, Pinchi* (Adi).

Distribution & Status. Apparently common, both in the hills and plains. In the mountain, occurs up to 2700 m elevation. Although Prater (1948) mentioned of its occurrence above 1525 m in the hills, it has been recorded in Mehao W.S. at *c.* 400 m (Chakraborty & Sen, 1991) and also found at less than 100 m elevation on flat plains.

Subspecies. 2a *T. m. micrura*. Nominate subspecies.

(4) **3. *Talpa leucura*** White-tailed mole
T. leucura Blyth, 1850: 215. TYPE-LOCALITY: Cherrapunji, Khasi Hills, Meghalaya (originally recorded as Assam), India.

Local Names. *Ûk-muk, Ûtonua* (A), *Kurt, Pinchi* (Adi).

Distribution & Status. Found in the hills and plains, south of the Brahmaputra R., i.e., in E. Arunachal Pradesh. Although Corbet & Hill (1992) mentioned of its occurrence above 1000 m in the hills, the species has been observed and photographed at 139 m elevation on flat terrain in Phillobari RF,Tinsukia district in E. Assam, not far from Arunachal Pradesh border (Choudhury, 1997c).

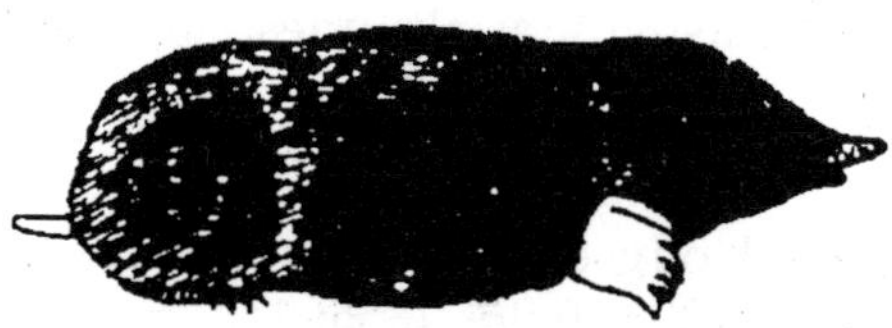

T. leucura

Remarks. Previously included as a subspecies of *T. micrura*. A distinctive species having a conspicuous white tail. It has three upper teeth on each side against four in *micrura*.

Family SORICIDAE

Shrews

Subfamily SORICINAE

4. *Sorex bedfordiae* Lesser stripe-backed shrew
S. bedfordiae Thomas, 1911a: 3 (and 1911b: 164). TYPE-LOCALITY: Omisan, Sichuan, China, 9500 ft.

Local Names. *Cheeka* (A, all shrews), *Pea* (Adi, all shrews).

Distribution & Status. Status in Arunachal Pradesh is unclear but its distribution from Nepal to China and N. Myanmar (Burma) along the Himalaya and other mountains indicate its presence in the state. A high elevation species usually occurring between 2100–4400 m.

(5) **5. *Soriculus nigrescens*** Sikkim large-clawed shrew
Corsira nigrescens Gray, 1842: 261. TYPE-LOCALITY: Darjeeling, West Bengal, India.

Distribution & Status. A high elevation species. Occurs in the higher hills and mountains, usually between 1500–4300 m elevation. Not uncommon in the *jhums* and cultivations.

Subspecies. 5a *S. n. radulus*
S. radulus Thomas, 1922b: 429. TYPE-LOCALITY: Dreyi, Mishmi Hills, Arunachal Pradesh (originally recorded as N. Assam), India, 5140 ft.

(6) **6. *Soriculus caudatus*** Hodgson's brown-toothed shrew
Sorex caudatus Horsfield, 1851: 135. TYPE-LOCALITY: Darjeeling, West Bengal, India.

Distribution & Status. A high elevation species. Occurs in the higher hills and mountains, usually at altitudes between 1800–3600 m.

Subspecies. 6a *S. c. caudatus.* Nominate subspecies.

(7) **7. *Soriculus leucops*** Hodgson's brown-toothed shrew
S. leucops Hodgson in Horsfield, 1855: 111. TYPE-LOCALITY: Nepal.

Distribution & Status. Recorded in Mishmi Hills. The western limit is in Nepal. Hence, its occurrence all over the state is apparent.

Subspecies. 7a *S. l. baileyi*
S. baileyi Thomas, 1914a: 683. TYPE-LOCALITY: Tsu R., Mishmi Hills, Arunachal Pradesh (originally recorded as Assam), India, 7500 ft.

Remarks. This subspecies was considered a race of *S. caudatus* (Ellerman & Morrison-Scott, 1951). Reviewed by Hoffmann (1986) and considered a race of *S. leucops*.

8. *Soriculus macrurus*
S. macrurus Blanford, 1888: 231. TYPE-LOCALITY: Darjeeling, West Bengal, India.

Distribution & Status. So far no specific record from Arunachal Pradesh but its occurrence along the Himalaya from Nepal eastwards (up to Sichuan, China) suggests its presence in the state.

Remarks. Osgood (1932) included it in *S. leucops* but is apparently very distinctive.

(8) **9. *Suncus murinus*** House, or Grey musk shrew
Sorex murinus Linnaeus, 1766: 74. TYPE-LOCALITY: Java, Indonesia.

Distribution & Status. Common throughout. In the Himalaya and Mishmi Hills, occurs below 2900 m.

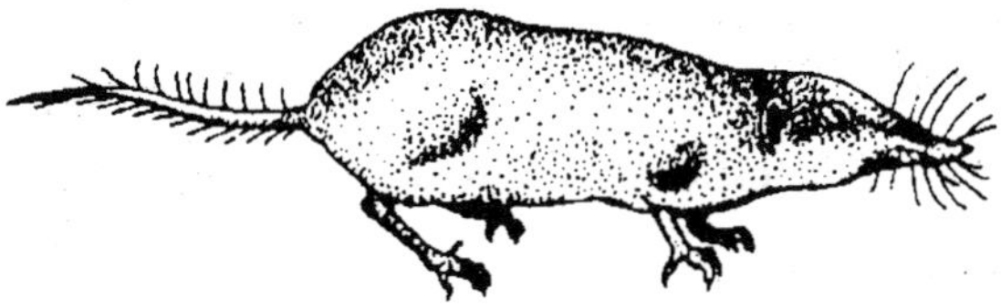

House shrew

Subspecies. 9a *S. m. murinus*. Nominate subspecies.
9b *S. m. soccatus*
Sorex soccatus Hodgson, 1845: 270. TYPE-LOCALITY: Central Nepal.
9c *S. m. griffithi*
Sorex griffithi Horsfield, 1851: 134. TYPE-LOCALITY: Probably Assam (Lindsay, 1929).
9d *S. m. fulvocinerea*
Crocidura (Pachyura) fulvocinerea Anderson, 1877: 263. TYPE-LOCALITY: Guwahati (Gauhati), Assam, India.

Remarks. The subspecies may be treated as tentative until a comprehensive review is undertaken. Corbet & Hill (1992) suggests *S. m. nemorivagus* as a subspecies possibly including *soccatus* and *griffithi*. One reason for confusion in subspecific variation is the translocation and introduction in different areas due to inadvertent man-made factors.

(9) **10. *Suncus etruscus*** Savi's pigmy shrew
Sorex etruscus Savi, 1822: 60. TYPE-LOCALITY: Pisa, Italy.

Distribution & Status. Occurs in the lower hills and foothills. Not uncommon.

Subspecies. 10a *S. e. nudipes*
Sorex nudipes Blyth, 1855: 34. TYPE-LOCALITY: Amherst, Tenasserim, Myanmar (Burma).
10b *S. e. pygmaeoides*
Crocidura (Pachyura) pygmaeoides Anderson, 1877: 279. TYPE-LOCALITY: Himalayas.

Remarks. The subspecific classification needs a comprehensive review.

(10) **11. *Crocidura attenuata*** Grey shrew
C. attenuata Milne-Edwards, 1872b: 231, pls 38B, 39A. TYPE-LOCALITY: Moupin, Sichuan, China.

Local Name. *Pea* (Adi).

Distribution & Status. Found throughout Arunachal Pradesh.

Subspecies. 11a *C. a. rubricosa*
C. rubricosa Anderson, 1877: 280. TYPE-LOCALITY: Sibsagar, Assam.

Remarks. The subspecific variation needs a comprehensive review.

12. ***Crocidura gueldenstaedtii***
Sorex güldenstaedtii Pallas, 1811: 132, pl. 9. TYPE-LOCALITY: Near Dushet, Georgia.

Distribution & Status. No specific record so far but likely to occur in the mountains, chiefly above 2000 m.

Remarks. Ellerman & Morrison-Scott (1951) included it in *C. russula*. Taxonomy still uncertain.

13. ***Crocidura horsfieldi*** Horsfield's shrew
Sorex horsfieldi Tomes, 1856: 23. TYPE-LOCALITY: Sri Lanka.

Distribution & Status. Found but exact status unclear.

Remarks. Ellerman & Morrison-Scott (1951) included it in *C. russula*.

(11) **14.** ***Anourosorex squamipes*** Mole-shrew, or Szechuan burrowing shrew
A. squamipes Milne-Edwards, 1872b: 264, pl. 38. TYPE-LOCALITY: ? Moupin, Sichuan, China.

Distribution & Status. Found all over from plains to the mountains, up to 3000 m. Earlier known to occur in the hills above 300 m (Corbet & Hill, 1992) but a specimen examined at Podumoni RF, Tinsukia district in E. Assam in 1993 on flat plains at an elevation of only 119 m (Choudhury, 1997e). At Gandhigram near Namdapha N.P., recorded at 1100 m elevation (Ghosh, 1987) while in Mehao W.S. recorded up to 1800 m (Chakraborty & Sen, 1991).

Remarks. The subspecific classification is still not concrete.

(12) **15.** ***Chimarrogale himalayica*** Himalayan water shrew
Crossopus himalayicus Gray, 1842: 261. TYPE-LOCALITY: Chamba, Himachal Pradesh (originally recorded as N.E. Punjab), India.

Distribution & Status. Found in the hills between 800–1500 m elevation.

Remarks. Earlier considered as a subspecies of *C. platycephala* (Ellerman & Morrison-Scott, 1951)

16. *Nectogale elegans*
N. elegans Milne-Edwards, 1870: 341. TYPE-LOCALITY: Moupin, Sichuan, China.

Distribution & Status. Found in the hills and mountains between 900–2300 m elevation.

Remarks. Haunts rivers and streams.

Order SCANDENTIA

Tree-shrews

Tree-shrews, which were included in the orders Primates and Insectivora, are now usually placed in a separate order Scandentia, which contains a single family, Tupaiidae. The uncertainty relating to the taxonomic status of the tree-shrews have been reviewed by Campbell (1974) and the contributors in Luckett (1980). The recent checklists of Corbet & Hill (1992) and Wilson & Reeder (1993) also placed it in this order. The tree-shrews are mostly arboreal, diurnal and are also omnivorous.

Tree-shrew

Family TUPAIIDAE

Tree-shrews

(13) **17. *Tupaia belangeri*** Northern tree-shrew
Cladobates belangeri Wagner, 1841: 42. TYPE-LOCALITY: Siriam, near Yangon (Rangoon), Myanmar (Burma).

Local Names. *Tei* (Adi).

Distribution & Status. Found all over, from plains to hills. Not uncommon. The subspecies *assamensis* is common in the Patkai Range (Tirap and Changlang districts) and Mishmi Hills (E. Siang, Dibang Valley and Lohit districts). Also perhaps in the Himalayas, west of the Siang R. The subspecies *lepcha* is probably found in W. Arunachal Pradesh. Its exact status is, however, still not clear.

Subspecies. 17a *T. b. assamensis* Wroughton, 1921a: 599. TYPE-LOCALITY: Mokokchung, Nagaland (originally recorded as Naga Hills, Assam), India.
17b *T. b. lepcha* Thomas, 1922a: 428. TYPE-LOCALITY: Narbong, near Darjeeling, West Bengal, India, 2000 ft.

Remarks. Except Agrawal (1975), no comprehensive review has been done on the subspecific variations. He also synonimised *T. b. versurae* (Thomas, 1922b: 428. TYPE-LOCALITY: Dening, Mishmi Hills, 2250 ft.) with *assamensis*. So long the species was mentioned as *T. glis* Diard, 1820 (Ellerman & Morrison-Scott, 1951; Prater, 1948; Choudhury, 1994a). In fact, *T. glis* which was described from Penang, Malaya, has its northern limit of distribution in southern Thailand. However, there has been no comprehensive review on the differences between the two species.

Order CHIROPTERA

Bats

The order Chiroptera comprises the Bats, the only mammal which can really fly like birds. Other flying mammals like the flying squirrels actually do not fly but glide. Bats are second only to the Rodentia in number of species in the world. Although found almost all over the globe, majority occur in the tropical and subtropical areas. The bats are divided into two suborders, one, the Megachiroptera or the Old World fruit bats, the other, the Microchiroptera, the predominantly insectivorous and carnivorous species. Of some 18 families, seven occur in Arunachal Pradesh. A comprehensive review on the bats is found in Miller (1907). Some recent reviews include those of Hill (1974), Van Valen (1979), and Koopman (1982–85, 1984, 1989).

Suborder MEGACHIROPTERA

Family PTEROPODIDAE

Old World fruit bats

Subfamily PTEROPODINAE

(14) **18. *Pteropus giganteus*** Indian flying fox
Vespertilio gigantea Brünnich, 1782: 43. TYPE-LOCALITY: Bengal, India.

Local Names. *Bâduli* (A, all bats).

Distribution & Status. Found all over, however, not common due to persecution. The nominate race probably occurs in W. Arunachal Pradesh, may be elsewhere also while the race *leucocephalus* is widespread all over.

Subspecies. 18a *P. g. giganteus.* Nominate race.
18b *P. g. leucocephalus*
P. leucocephalus Hodgson, 1835a: 700. TYPE-LOCALITY: Central Nepal.

Remarks. The species is rare in the state. The exact distribution and status at subspecific level is not clear. WPA: Schedule V.

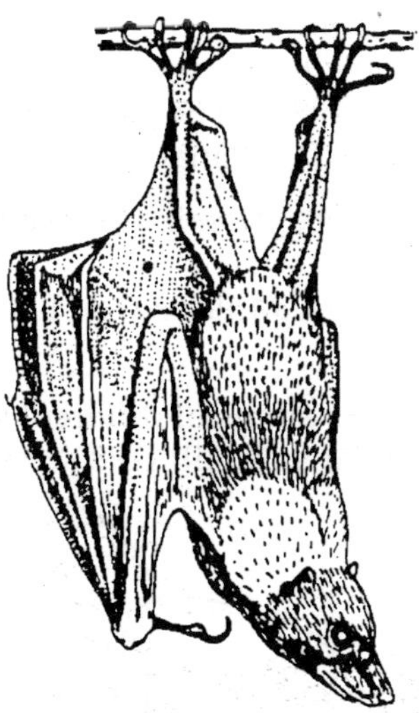

Flying fox

(15) **19. *Rousettus leschenaulti*** Fulvous fruit bat
Pteropus leschenaulti Desmarest, 1820: 110. TYPE-LOCALITY: Pondicherry, India.

Distribution & Status. A wide ranging species. Although found, its extact status is unclear. Specimen record from Namdapha N.P. (Ghosh, 1987) and Mehao W.S. (Chakraborty & Sen, 1991).

(16) **20. *Cynopterus brachyotis*** Lesser dog-faced fruit bat
Pachysoma brachyotis Müller, 1838: 146. TYPE-LOCALITY: Dewei R., Borneo.

Distribution & Status. Recorded as common up to 1800 m elevation in Mehao W.S. (Chakraborty & Sen, 1991). Status elsewhere is unclear but likely to occur.

Remarks. The subspecies *angulatus* Miller, 1898, which was considered a race of *brachyotis* (Ellerman & Morrison-Scott, 1951) is now found to be specifically indistinct from *C. sphinx* (Corbet & Hill, 1992).

(17) **21. *Cynopterus sphinx*** Short-nosed bat
Vespertilio sphinx Vahl, 1797: 123. TYPE-LOCALITY: Tranquebar, Tamil Nadu (Madras), India.

Distribution & Status. Common all over the area, both plains and hills. The subspecies *angulatus* was first recorded in India in Namdapha N.P. (Ghosh 1987). The nominate race has also been recorded in Namdapha N.P. (Vanak & Goyal 1996).

Subspecies. 21a *C. s. sphinx*. Nominate race.
21b *C. s. angulatus*
C. angulatus Miller, 1898: 316. Miller's fruit bat. TYPE-LOCALITY: Trong, S. Thailand.

Remarks. Distribution and status of different subspecies is unclear. Hill & Thonglongya (1972) and Hill (1983) reviewed its taxonomic history.

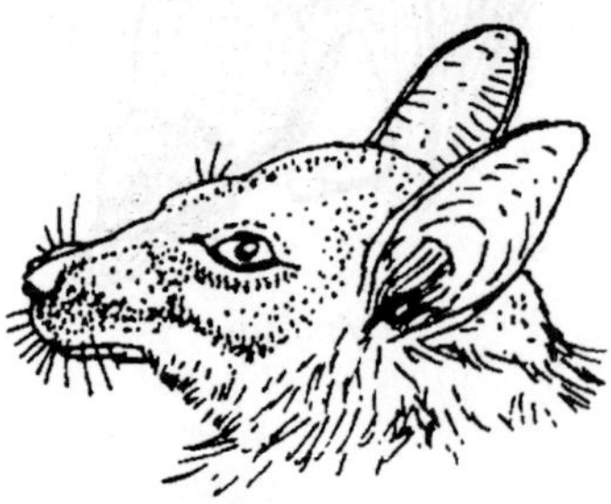

C. brachyotis

(18) **22. *Megaerops niphanae*** Tail-less fruit bat
M. niphanae Yenbutra & Felten, 1983: 2. TYPE-LOCALITY: Amphoe Pak Thong Chai, Nakon Ratchasima Prov., Thailand, 14°30′ N., 101°56′ E.

Distribution & Status. Found, probably all over in the hills and mountains. Specimen record from Namdapha N.P., Changlang district (then a part of Tirap district; Saha, 1984).

Remarks. The distribution pattern of *M. niphanae* and *M. ecaudatus* suggests that the earlier references of latter species by Hill (1983) and Saha (1984) from north-eastern India were in all probability belonged to the former species.

23. *Sphaerias blanfordi* Blanford's, or Mountain fruit bat
Cynopterus blanfordi Thomas, 1891: 884. TYPE-LOCALITY: Leito, Cheba, Karen Hills, Burma (Myanmar), 1000 m.

Distribution & Status. Found but exact status unclear. Recorded at Gandhigram near Namdapha N.P. (Ghosh, 1987).

Subspecies. 23a *S. b. motuoensis* Cai & Zhang, 1980: 443. TYPE-LOCALITY: Beibing, Motuo region, S. Tibet.

Remarks. The type-locality of the subspecies *motuoensis* is near the India-China international boundary.

Subfamily MACROGLOSSINAE

(19) **24. *Eonycteris spelaea*** Dawn, or Cave fruit bat
Macroglossus spelaeus Dobson, 1871a: 105, 106; 1871b: 261. TYPE-LOCALITY: Farm Caves, Moulmein, Tenasserim, Myanmar (Burma).

Distribution & Status. Found but exact status unclear.

(20) **25. *Macroglossus sobrinus*** Long-tongued hill fruit bat
M. minimus sobrinus Anderson, 1911: 641, 642. TYPE-LOCALITY: Mt. Igari, Perak, Malaya (Malaysia).

Distribution & Status. Specifically recorded from Namdapha N.P. (Saha, 1985, as *M. minimus*).

Suborder MICROCHIROPTERA

Family EMBALLONURIDAE

Sheath-tailed bats

(21) **26. *Taphozous melanopogon*** Black-bearded tomb bat
T. melanopogon Temminck, 1841: 287. TYPE-LOCALITY: Bantam, W. Java, Indonesia.

Distribution & Status. Found but status unclear.

(22) **27. *Taphozous longimanus*** Long-winged tomb bat
T. longimanus Hardwicke, 1825b: 525. TYPE-LOCALITY: Calcutta, India.

Distribution & Status. Found but exact status unclear.

(23) **28. *Taphozous nudiventris*** Naked-rumped tomb bat
T. nudiventris Cretzschmar, 1830–1831: 70. TYPE-LOCALITY: Egypt.

Distribution & Status. Status unclear but present.

Remarks. Ellerman & Morrison-Scott (1951) listed it as *Taphozous kachhensis* Dobson, 1872c: 221.

(24) **29. *Taphozous saccolaimus*** Pouch-bearing bat
T. saccolaimus Temminck, 1838: 14. TYPE-LOCALITY: Java, Indonesia. Lectotype designated by Tate (1941).

Distribution & Status. Status unclear but present.

Family MEGADERMATIDAE

False vampire bats

(25) **30. *Megaderma spasma*** Lesser false vampire bat
Vespertilio spasma Linnaeus, 1758: 32 (based on Seba, 1734: 90, pl. 56, fig. 1). TYPE-LOCALITY: Ternate I, Moluccas, Indonesia.

Distribution & Status. Found but exact status not known.

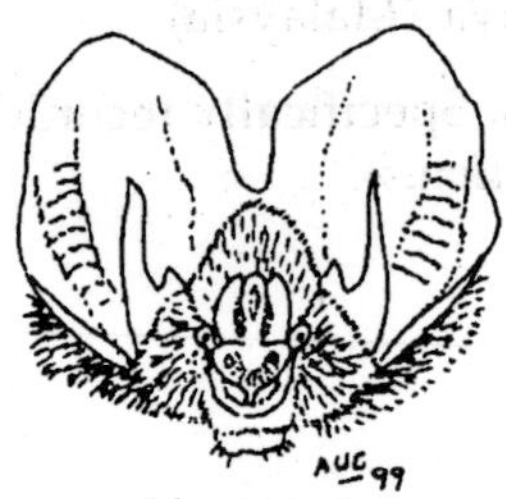

M. spasma

(26) **31. *Megaderma lyra*** Greater, or Indian false vampire
M. lyra Geoffroy, 1810b: 190. TYPE-LOCALITY: India (? east coast, Madras, Tamil Nadu).

Distribution & Status. Found all over the state. Common at places.

Family RHINOLOPHIDAE

Horseshoe bats

(27) **32. *Rhinolophus trifoliatus*** Trefoil horseshoe bat
R. trifoliatus Temminck, 1834: 24, pl. 1 (and 1835: 27, pl. 31). TYPE-LOCALITY: Bantam, W. Java, Indonesia.

Distribution & Status. No specific record but very likely to occur.

(28) **33. *Rhinolophus luctus*** Woolly horseshoe bat
R. luctus Temminck, 1834: 23, pl. 1 (and 1835: 24, pl. 30). TYPE-LOCALITY: Tapos, Java, Indonesia.

Distribution & Status. An uncommon species found all over.

34. *Rhinolophus macrotis* Big-eared horshoe bat
R. macrotis Blyth, 1844: 485. TYPE-LOCALITY: Nepal.

Distribution & Status. Known from Namdapha N.P. (Bates & Harrison, 1997).

Remarks. IUCN: DD.

(30) **35. *Rhinolophus yunanensis***
R. yunanensis Dobson, 1872a: 336. TYPE-LOCALITY: Hotha, Yunnan, China.

Distribution & Status. Specific record from Dening, Mishmi Hills in Lohit district (erroneously recorded as 'Mishmi Hills, Meghalaya' by Hill, 1986, but corrected by Choudhury, 1989e). Considering its range which extends from Meghalaya to Thailand and S.E. China, it probably occurs in other parts of Arunachal Pradesh also.

Remarks. IUCN: LR (nt).

(31) **36. *Rhinolophus lepidus*** Blyth's horseshoe bat
R. lepidus Blyth, 1844: 486. TYPE-LOCALITY: ? Calcutta, India (also see Das, 1986).

Distribution & Status. Occurs widely in the state.

(32) **37. *Rhinolophus pusillus*** Least horseshoe bat
R. minor Horsfield, 1823: pt. 6, pl. TYPE-LOCALITY: Java, Indonesia. Pre-occupied by *Vespertilio ferrumequinum minor* Kerr, 1792.

Distribution & Status. Widespread all over.

(33) **38. *Rhinolophus subbadius***
R. subbadius Blyth, 1844: 486. TYPE-LOCALITY: Nepal.

Distribution & Status. Specimen from Kalaktang, W. Kameng dist. (Bates & Harrison, 1997).

Remarks. IUCN: DD.

(34) **39. *Rhinolophus rouxii*** Rufous horseshoe bat
R. rouxii Temminck, 1835: 30b. TYPE-LOCALITY: Pondicherry and Calcutta, India.

Distribution & Status. Found all over Arunachal Pradesh. A wide-ranging species, occurs from Sri Lanka to S. China and Indonesia.

(35) **40. *Rhinolophus affinis*** Intermediate horseshoe bat
R. affinis Horsfield, 1823: pt. 6, pl. TYPE-LOCALITY: Java, Indonesia.

Distribution & Status. Widely distributed all over.

(36) **41. *Rhinolophus ferrumequinum*** Greater horseshoe bat
Vespertilio ferrumequinum Schreber, 1774: pl. 62. TYPE-LOCALITY: France.

Distribution & Status. Known from Dening in Mishmi Hills, Lohit dist (Hinton & Lindsay, 1926). However, considering its extensive distribution range, it is likely to occur widely.

Remarks. IUCN: LR (nt).

Family HIPPOSIDERIDAE

Old-World leaf-nosed bats, Trident bats

(37) **42. *Hipposideros pomona***
H. pomona Anderson, 1918: 380, 381. TYPE-LOCALITY: Haleri, N. Coorg, Karnataka, India.

Distribution & Status. Widespread all over.

Remarks. Earlier thought to be conspecific with *H. bicolor*, however, Hill *et al.*, (1986) recognised it as a separate species. Included as *H. bicolor* in Choudhury (1994a). IUCN: DD.

(40) **43. *Hipposideros cineraceus*** Least leaf-nosed bat
Hipposideros cineraceus Blyth, 1853: 410. TYPE-LOCALITY: Punjab, Pakistan.

Distribution & Status. Known only from 'Tiki' (Hinton & Lindsay, 1926).

(39) **44. *Hipposideros fulvus*** Fulvous leaf-nosed bat
H. fulvus Gray, 1838: 492. TYPE-LOCALITY: 'Madras', actually apparently Dharwar, Karnataka, India.

Distribution & Status. Found but exact status unclear.

(42) **45. *Hipposideros armiger*** Himalayan leaf-nosed bat
Rhinolophus armiger Hodgson, 1835a: 699. TYPE-LOCALITY: Nepal.

Distribution & Status. Widespread all over, especially in the foothills and hills.

(43) **46. *Hipposideros larvatus***
Rhinolophus larvatus Horsfield, 1823: pt. 6, pl. TYPE-LOCALITY: Java, Indonesia.

Distribution & Status. Recorded in Mehao W.S. (Chakraborty & Sen, 1991). No record from other parts of Arunachal Pradesh so far, however, specimen record from Khasi Hills, Meghalaya (recorded as Assam, as till 1972, Khasi Hills formed part of Assam). Likely to occur all over as it has been recorded throughout the S.E. Asia including N. Myanmar (Burma).

Subspecies. 46a *H. l. leptophylla*
Phyllorhina leptophylla Dobson, 1874: 234. TYPE-LOCALITY: Khasi Hills, Assam (now Meghalaya), India.

47. *Hipposideros lankadiva* Large leaf-nosed bat
H. lankadiva Kelaart, 1850: 216. TYPE-LOCALITY: Kandy, Sri Lanka.

Distribution & Status. Recorded only from Namdapha N.P. (Ghosh, 1987). Mainly a species of peninsular India.

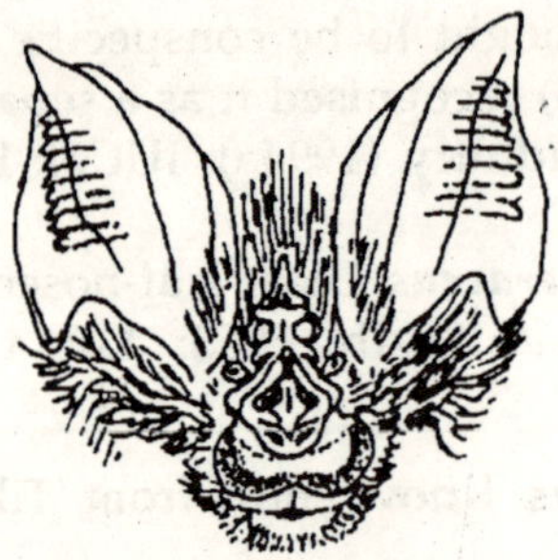

Rhinolophus luctus

Family VESPERTILIONIDAE

Evening bats

Subfamily VESPERTILIONINAE

48. ***Myotis sicarius***
M. sicarius Thomas, 1915c: 608. TYPE-LOCALITY: N. Sikkim, India.

Distribution & Status. Occurs but exact status unclear. IUCN: VU.

(45) **49.** ***Myotis formosus*** Hodgson's bat
Vespertilio formosa Hodgson, 1835a: 700. TYPE-LOCALITY: Nepal.

Distribution & Status. Although not specifically recorded from Arunachal Pradesh, the species occurs from Nepal to Philippines with specimen records from north Bengal also. Hence, very likely to occur.

(46) **50.** ***Myotis siligorensis*** Himalayan whiskered bat
Vespertilio siligorensis Horsfield, 1855: 102. TYPE-LOCALITY: Siligori, Nepal (perhaps Siliguri, now in West Bengal, India).

Distribution & Status. Occurs but exact status unclear.

(47) **51.** ***Myotis mystacinus*** Whiskered bat
Vespertilio mystacinus Kuhl, 1819: 202. TYPE-LOCALITY: Germany.

Distribution & Status. Found but exact status unclear.

(48) **52.** ***Myotis muricola***
Vespertilio tralatitius Temminck, 1840: 228, pl. 57. TYPE-LOCALITY: Java, Indonesia. Preoccupied by *V. tralatitius* Horsfield, 1824.

Distribution & Status. Found all over, both plains and hills.

(49) **53. *Myotis annectans*** Hairy-faced bat
Pipistrellus annectans Dobson, 1871c: 213. TYPE-LOCALITY: Naga Hills, (now Nagaland, originally recorded as Assam), India.

Distribution & Status. No specific record from Arunachal Pradesh but specimens recorded from Darjeeling as well as Thailand besides the type locality suggesting its possible occurrence.

Remarks. Recognised as *Pipistrellus annectans* in Ellerman & Morrison-Scott (1951). Reviewed by Topal (1970) who included it in the genus *Myotis*. IUCN: LR (nt)

(50) **54. *Myotis daubentonii*** Daubenton's bat, Water bat
Vespertilio daubentonii Kuhl, 1819: 195. TYPE-LOCALITY: Hanau, Hessen-Nassau, Germany.

Distribution & Status. Found but exact status unclear.

(51) **55. *Barbastella leucomelas*** Eastern barbastelle
Vespertilio leucomelas Cretzschmar, 1830 or 1831: 73, pl. 18b. TYPE-LOCALITY: Arabia Petraea (=Sinai, Egypt).

Distribution & Status. Status unclear, but found.

Subspecies. 55a *B.l. darjelingensis*
Plecotus darjelingensis Hodgson, in Horsfield, 1855: 103. TYPE-LOCALITY: Darjeeling, West Bengal, India.

(52) **56. *Scotomanes ornatus*** Harlequin bat
Nycticejus ornatus Blyth, 1851b: 517. TYPE-LOCALITY: Cherrapunji, Khasi Hills, Meghalaya (originally recorded as Assam), India.

Distribution & Status. Dening in Mishmi Hills (Hinton & Lindsay, 1926).

Subspecies. 56a *S. o. ornatus.* Nominate subspecies.
56b *S. o. imbrensis* Thomas, 1921c: 772. TYPE-LOCALITY: Khonshnong, Jaintia Hills, Meghalaya (originally recorded as Assam), India, 3000 ft.

Remarks. IUCN: LR (nt).

(53) **57. *Scotophilus kuhlii*** Asiatic lesser yellow house bat
S. kuhlii Leach, 1821: 72. TYPE-LOCALITY: Unknown.

Distribution & Status. Status unclear but occurs widely.

Remarks. Previously referred to as *Scotophilus temminckii* Horsfield, 1824: pt. 8. Reviewed by Hill (in Peterson, 1968) and Hill & Thonglongya (1972).

(54) **58. *Scotophilus heathii*** Asiatic greater yellow house bat
S. heathii Horsfield, 1831: 113. TYPE-LOCALITY: Madras, Tamil Nadu, India.

Distribution & Status. Recorded in Mehao W.S. where it is common in the lower elevations and opener areas (Chakraborty & Sen, 1991). Status elsewhere is unclear but likely to occur.

(55) **59. *Eptesicus pachyotis*** Thick-eared bat
Vesperugo (Vesperus) pachyotis Dobson, 1871c: 211. TYPE-LOCALITY: Khasi Hills, Meghalaya (originally recorded as Assam), India.

Distribution & Status. No specific record from Arunachal Pradesh so far, however, likely to occur. IUCN: LR (nt).

(56) **60. *Tylonycteris pachypus*** Bamboo bat, Flat-headed bat, Club-footed bat
Vespertilio pachypus Temminck, 1840: 217, pl. 54. TYPE-LOCALITY: Bantam, W. Java, Indonesia.

Distribution & Status. Widespread all over.

Subspecies. 60a *T.p. fulvidus*
Scotophilus fulvidus Blyth, 1859: 293. TYPE-LOCALITY: Schwegyin, R. Sittang, S.E. Burma (Myanmar). Needs a review.

(57) **61. *Pipistrellus ceylonicus*** Kelaart's pipistrelle
Scotophilus ceylonicus Kelaart, 1852: 22. TYPE-LOCALITY: Trincomalee, Sri Lanka.
Local Names. *Chûnga-bâduli* (A, all small bats including pipistrelles).

Distribution & Status. No record but likely to occur as its range indicates.

Remarks. The Indian population have been reviewed by Lal (1984) and only one subspecies, *P. c. indicus* has been proposed.

(58) **62. *Pipistrellus paterculus***
P. paterculus Thomas, 1915b: 32. TYPE-LOCALITY: Mount Popa, N. Burma (Myanmar).

Distribution & Status. Status unclear but present.

Remarks. Tentatively considered as a subspecies of *P. abramus* (Ellerman & Morrison-Scott, 1951). IUCN: LR (nt).

(59) **63. *Pipistrellus javanicus*** Javan pipistrelle
Scotophilus javanicus Gray, 1838: 498. TYPE-LOCALITY: Java, Indonesia.

Distribution & Status. Well distributed all over Arunachal Pradesh.

Remarks. *P. babu* Thomas, 1915b, which was considered a distinct species (Ellerman & Morrison-Scott, 1951) has been synonymised with *P. javanicus* (Corbet & Hill, 1992).

(60) **64. *Pipistrellus coromandra*** Indian pipistrelle
Scotophilus coromandra Gray, 1838: 498. TYPE-LOCALITY: Pondicherry, Coromandel coast, India.

Distribution & Status. Found all over, not uncommon.

P. coromandra

(61) **65. *Pipistrellus tenuis*** Least pipistrelle
Vespertilio tenuis Temminck, 1840: 229. TYPE-LOCALITY: Sumatra, Indonesia (Tate, 1942).

Distribution & Status. Distributed all over Arunachal Pradesh.

Subspecies. 65a *P. t. mimus*
P. mimus Wroughton, 1899: 722. TYPE-LOCALITY: Mheskatri, Dangs, Gujarat, India.
65b *P. t. principulus*
P. principulus Thomas, 1915a: 231. TYPE-LOCALITY: Gauhati (Guwahati), Assam, India.

Remarks. *P. mimus* was considered earlier as a distinct species (Ellerman & Morrison-Scott, 1951). The subspecific classification needs review.

(62) **66. *Pipistrellus savii*** Savi's pipistrelle
Vespertilio savii Bonaparte, 1837: fasc. 20. TYPE-LOCALITY: Pisa, Italy.

Distribution & Status. No record but likely to occur as its range indicates.

Subspecies. 66a *P. s. austenianus*

? *P. austenianus* Dobson, 1871c: 213. TYPE-LOCALITY: Cherrapunji, Khasi Hills, Meghalaya (originally recorded as Assam), India.

(63) **67. *Pipistrellus cadornae*** Cadorna's pipistrelle
P. cadornae Thomas, 1916a: 416. TYPE-LOCALITY: Pashok, Darjeeling, West Bengal, India, 3500 ft.

Distribution & Status. No record but likely to occur as its range indicates.

Remarks. Earlier considered as a subspecies of *P. savii* (Ellerman & Morrison-Scott, 1951). Treated as a distinct species by Corbet & Hill (1992). IUCN: LR (nt).

(64) **68. *Pipistrellus affinis*** Chocolate bat
Vesperugo (Pipistrellus) affinis Dobson, 1871c: 213. TYPE-LOCALITY: Bhamo, N.E. Burma (Myanmar).

Distribution & Status. No record but likely to occur as its range indicates.

Remarks. Erroneously listed as *mordax* by Wroughton (1916b, 1918) and Ellerman & Morrison-Scott (1951) (Francis & Hill, 1986).

(66) **69. *Nyctalus noctula*** Common noctule
Vespertilio noctula Schreber, 1774: 166, pl. 52. TYPE-LOCALITY: France.

Distribution & Status. Exact status unclear but present.

Subspecies. 69a *N. n. labiatus*
Vespertilio labiata Hodgson, 1835a: 700. TYPE-LOCALITY: Nepal.

(67) **70. *Hesperoptenus tickelli*** Tickell's bat
Nycticejus tickelli Blyth, 1851a: 157. TYPE-LOCALITY: 'central India, Ceylon and the intervening hilly country'; restricted to Chaibassa, Bihar by Anderson (1881) and Wroughton (1918).

Distribution & Status. No specimen record so far but likely to occur.

Subfamily MINIOPTERINAE

(68) **71. *Miniopterus schreibersii*** Schreibers' long-fingered bat
Vespertilio schreibersii Kuhl, 1819: 185. TYPE-LOCALITY: 'Columbäzar Höhle', R. Danube, Romania.

Distribution & Status. Found all over.

Remarks. IUCN: LR (nt).

(69) **72. *Miniopterus pusillus***
M. pusillus Dobson, 1876: 162. TYPE-LOCALITY: Nicobar Is (Wroughton, 1918; Hill, 1983).

Distribution & Status. No specimen record but likely to occur.

Subfamily MURININAE

Tube-nosed bats

(70) **73. *Murina leucogaster*** Greater tube-nosed bat
M. leucogaster Milne-Edwards, 1872b: 252, pls. 37b, 37c. TYPE-LOCALITY: Moupin district, Sichuan, China.

Distribution & Status. No specific record but likely to occur.

(71) **74. *Murina aurata*** Little tube-nosed bat
M. aurata Milne-Edwards, 1872b: 250, pls. 37b, 37c. TYPE-LOCALITY: Moupin, Sichuan, China.

Distribution & Status. Recorded from Namdapha N.P. (Ghosh, 1987). Apparently found in other areas of eastern Arunachal Pradesh as there are records from sites in Tibet and N. Myanmar (Burma) which are close to Indian border.

Remarks. IUCN: LR (nt).

(72) **75. *Murina tubinaris***
Harpiocephalus tubinaris Scully, 1881: 200. TYPE-LOCALITY: Gilgit, Kashmir.

Distribution & Status. In Lohit dist, at Dening (Hinton & Lindsay, 1926).

Remarks. Ellerman & Morrison-Scott (1951) listed it as a subspecies of *M. huttoni.*

(73) **76. *Murina huttonii*** Hutton's tube-nosed bat
Harpiocephalus huttonii Peters, 1872: 257. TYPE-LOCALITY: Dehra Dun, Kumaon, Uttar Pradesh, India.

Distribution & Status. No record but likely to occur as its range indicates.

Remarks. IUCN: LR (nt).

(74) **77. *Murina cyclotis*** Orange tube-nosed bat, Round-eared tube-nosed bat
M. cyclotis Dobson, 1872b: 210. TYPE-LOCALITY: Darjeeling, West Bengal, India.

Distribution & Status. No record but likely to occur as its range indicates.

Subspecies. 77a *M. c. cyclotis*. Nominate race.

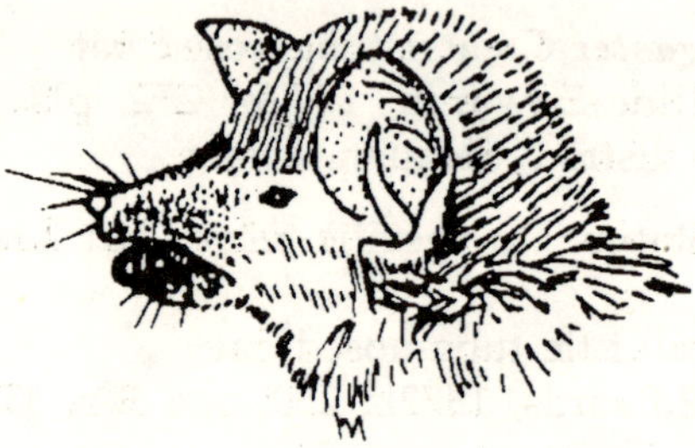

M. cyclotis

(75) **78. *Harpiocephalus harpia*** Hairy-winged bat
Vespertilio harpia Temminck, 1840: 219, pl. 55. TYPE-LOCALITY: South-eastern side of Mt. Gede, Java, Indonesia. Lectotype designated by Husson (1955).

Distribution & Status. No record but likely to occur as its range indicates.

Subspecies. 78a *H. h. lasyura*
Noctulinia lasyura Hodgson, 1847b: 896. TYPE-LOCALITY: 'central hills, sub Himalayas', restricted to Darjeeling, West Bengal by Wroughton (1918).

Subfamily KERIVOULINAE

79. *Kerivoula picta* Painted bat
Vespertilio pictus Pallas, 1767: 7. TYPE-LOCALITY: Probably Moluccas, Indonesia.

Kerivoula sp.

Distribution & Status. Recorded from adjacent Lakhimpur in Assam (Chaturvedi, 1969).

Family MOLOSSIDAE

Free-tailed bats

(77) **80. *Tadarida teniotis*** European free-tailed bat
Cephalotes teniotis Rafinesque, 1814: 12. TYPE-LOCALITY: Sicily, Italy.

Distribution & Status. No record but likely to occur all over Arunachal Pradesh as its range indicates.

(78) **81. *Tadarida plicata*** Wrinkle-lipped free-tailed bat
Vespertilio plicatus Buchannan, 1800: 261, pl. 13. TYPE-LOCALITY: Bengal, India.

Distribution & Status. A widespread species occurring from W. India to Philippines. Likely to occur all over Arunachal Pradesh.

Order PRIMATES

Primates

The natural order, the Primates or the first, or highest of animals, contains the apes, monkeys and lemurs, and of course, the man. Most primates have comparatively superior development of the brain and have higher intelligence than other animals. Primates are characterised by large, forward-facing eyes; complete post-orbital bar and large brain. Most non-human primates are arboreal creatures, however, some spend a great deal of time on the ground also. In primates, the arrangement of the thumb is opposite to other fingers. The primates are divided into two suborders, Prosimii and the Anthropoidea. The former includes the primitive primates like the lemurs and lorises, the latter comprises the apes and monkeys, and also men. Of the 11 families commonly recognised, three are represented in Arunachal Pradesh, they are the loris (Loridae), monkeys (Cercopithecidae), and the ape (Hylobatidae). There are two subfamilies of Cercopithecidae, they are Cercopithecinae (macaques) and Colobinae (langurs). The tree-shrews are no longer considered as Primates.

Suborder PROSIMII

Family LORIDAE (Lorisidae)

Lorises

(79) **82.** ***Nycticebus coucang*** Slow loris
Tardigradus coucang Boddaert, 1785: 67. TYPE-LOCALITY: Bengal.

Local Names. *Lajuki bandor*(A), *Senni* (Adi), *Rangchubi* (Tangsa), *Awe* (Wancho).

Distribution & Status. In the forested hills and foothills. More common in the eastern areas, especially in Changlang Tirap, Lohit, and Dibang Valley districts.Elsewhere, found in W. and E. Kameng, Lower and Upper Subansiri, Papum Pare, W. and E. Siang districts. Protected areas where the species has been recorded are Mehao W.S., Namdapha N.P., Kane W.S., Itanagar W.S., Kamlang W.S., and Pakhui W.S. Also reported from Mouling N.P. In the mountains, recorded up to 2400 m elevation in Mehao W.S. (AUC).

Slow loris

Remarks. There is some confusion regarding subspecific classification. Ellerman & Morrison-Scott (1951) mentioned that the type-locality of the species is unknown (probably Malacca [Chasen]) suggesting that the nominate race occurs in Malaya and Sumatra. According to them, the subspecies found in India is *N. c. bengalensis* Fischer, 1804: 30. However, Corbet & Hill (1992) stated that the type-locality of the species is Bengal, thus indicating that the Indian animals are of nominate subspecies.

Distribution map in Corbet & Hill (1992) was not correct so far as N.E. India and N. Myanmar are concerned. CITES: Appendix II; WPA: Schedule I. IUCN: DD.

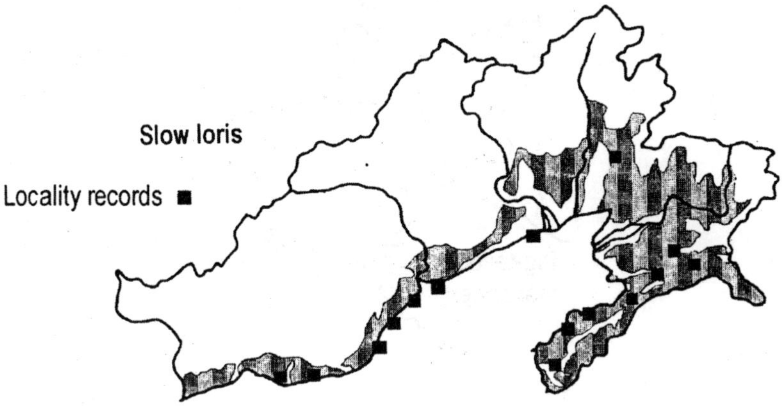

Suborder ANTHROPOIDEA

Family CERCOPITHECIDAE

Old-world monkeys

Subfamily CERCOPITHECINAE

Macaques

(80) **83. *Macaca nemestrina*** Pig-tailed macaque
Simia nemestrina Linnaeus, 1766: 35. TYPE-LOCALITY: Sumatra, Indonesia.

Distribution & Status. Found in the forests, both plains and hills, in the south bank of the Brahmaputra R. The species is not found in the north bank (Choudhury, 1989f). In Arunachal Pradesh, it is found in Dibang Valley, Lohit, Tirap and Changlang districts. Protected areas where the species has been recorded are Namdapha N.P., Mehao W.S. and Kamlang W.S.

Subspecies. 83a *M. n. leonina*
M. leoninus Blyth, 1863: 7. TYPE-LOCALITY: N. Arakan, Burma (Myanmar).

Remarks. The subspecies *M. n. blythii* Pocock, 1931: 305, has been synonymised by Fooden (1975). Its type-locality was unknown and the characteristics resembled those of *leonina.* Corbet & Hill (1992) did not include Arunachal Pradesh as well as N.E. India within the range of this species although its occurrence has been mentioned

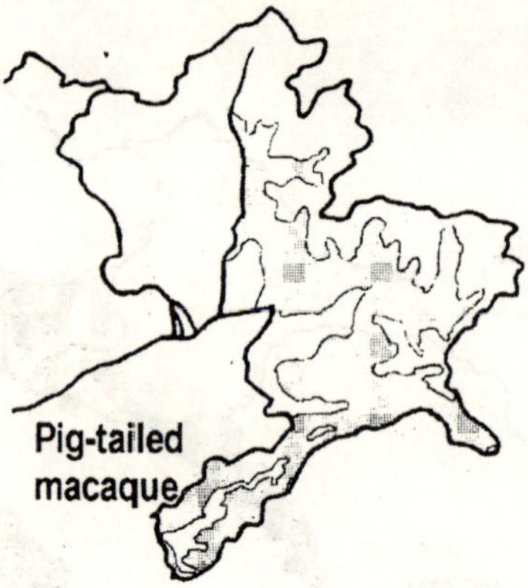

in Ellerman & Morrison-Scott (1951) and Choudhury (1988a, 1989f, 1994a, 1995a). IUCN: VU; WPA: Schedule II (I).

(81) **84. *Macaca assamensis*** Assamese macaque
M. assamensis McClelland, 1839: 148. TYPE-LOCALITY: Arunachal Pradesh (originally recorded as Assam), India.

Local Names. (All macaques/monkeys in general). *Shofu* (Aka), *Sibi bidé* (Apatani), *Sebe* (Bangni/Nishi), *Stung* (Bugun), *Ame* (Idu Mishmi), *Shubo* (Miji), *Prah, Zala* (Monpa).

Distribution & Status. Found in the dense forest, all over. In the mountains up to 2800 m elevation. May also occur at slightly higher areas in summer. The nominate subspecies, *M. a. assamensis,* is found in the forests, both plains and hills, S. of the Brahmaputra R., in E. Siang, Dibang Valley, Lohit, Tirap and Changlang districts. Protected areas having this subspecies are Namdapha N.P., Mehao W.S. and Kamlang W.S.

The subspecies *M. a. pelops* occurs only in the N. bank of the Brahmaputra R. (Choudhury, 1994a). Confined to the dense forests of Himalayan foothills and middle ranges, in the districts of Tawang, W. Kameng, E. Kameng, Lower Subansiri, Upper Subansiri, W. Siang, Upper Siang and E. Siang. Protected areas where this subspecies has been recorded are Mouling N.P., Kane W.S., Taley Valley W.S., Itanagar W.S., Pakhui W.S., Eaglenest W.S. and Sessa Orchid Sanctuary.

Subspecies. 84a *M. a. assamensis*. The nominate race. It is characterised by comparatively shorter tail (in adult males, 25–45% of head & body).
84b *M. a. pelops*
M. pelops Hodgson, 1841d: 1213. TYPE-LOCALITY: N. Nepal. The adult males have comparatively longer tail (50–63% of head & body).

Remarks. Distribution map in Corbet & Hill (1992) not correctly shown for N.E. India. The species has been observed at 100 m elevation also in Assam (Choudhury, 1996d). IUCN: VU; WPA: Schedule II (I).

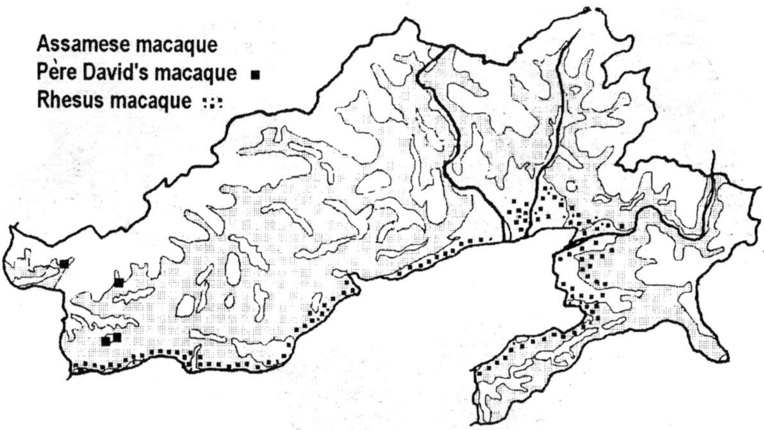

[***Macaca thibetana*** Père David's macaque, Tibetan macaque
Macacus thibetanus Milne-Edwards, 1870: 341. TYPE-LOCALITY: 20 km N. N.W. of Moupin (= Baoxing), Sichuan, China.

Distribution & Status. Macaques resembling this species and tentatively identified so were recorded for the first time near Lamacamp in W. Kameng dist in November, 1997 (Choudhury, 1998b) at an elevation of 2400 m. The location was just outside Eaglenest W.S. and Sessa Orchid Sanctuary. Also reported from northern areas of W. Kameng and Tawang districts.

Remarks. These interesting macaques were similar to *M. assamensis* but had some interesting variations. They had proportionately shorter tail (adult males having very short ones), slightly more prominent buffy side-whiskers and also slightly different ('heavy') vocalisation. It is intriguing whether the new macaque is *M. thibetana* or an undescribed subspecies of *M. assamensis*, or even a subspecies of the former? It was not *M. assamensis pelops*, which

Macaques found in Arunachal Pradesh, illustrating different characteristics. Rhesus (top left), pig-tailed (top right), Assamese (centre left), stump-tailed (centre right), possible Père David's (bottom).

occurs in the area. These interesting macaques need further study and a fresh review of *M. assamensis* and *thibetana*, at least at subspecific level is necessary (Choudhury, 2000a). Some authorities suggest it to be a subspecies of the former (Corbet & Hill, 1992).]

(82) **85. *Macaca mulatta*** Rhesus macaque, Rhesus monkey
Cercopithecus mulatta Zimmermann, 1780: 195. TYPE-LOCALITY: 'India'.

Local Names. (All macaques/monkeys in general). *Bândor* (A), *Sibe* (Adi), *Betam* (large macaque, Bangni/Nishi), *Bera* (smaller macaque, Bangni/Nishi), *Woi* (Singpho), *Voi* (Tangsa), *Mainak* (Wancho).

Distribution & Status. Although it is the most abundant primate of the region, in Arunachal Pradesh it is rare and confined to the foothills and adjacent plains only.

Subspecies. 85a. *M. m. mulatta*. The nominate race. The subspecific variation is insignificant and may be treated as tentative.

Remarks. The records from Thingbu area of Tawang district (Singh, 1991) were misidentified *M. assamensis*. IUCN: LR (nt); WPA: Schedule II (I).

(83) **86. *Macaca arctoides*** Stump-tailed macaque
Macacus arctoides Geoffroy, 1831: 61. TYPE-LOCALITY: 'Cochinchina', Vietnam.

Distribution & Status. Very rare. Restricted to the dense hill forests, south of the Brahmaputra R. Like *M. nemestrina*, it is not found north of the river (Choudhury, 1989f, 1996d). Small populations survive in Lohit, Tirap and Changlang districts. Presence suspected in Dibang Valley dist. Protected areas where the species is found are Namdapha N.P., Kamlang W.S., and Mehao W.S. (suspected). Also recorded from the floodplains near Namsai in Lohit dist. (Bhargava, 1988). Some of the reserved forests where it has been recorded or reported are Turung, Manabum, Tengapani, Kamlang (Lohit dist.), Miao, Pangsau, Diyun, Namphuk (Changlang dist.), Borduria and Namsang (Tirap dist.).

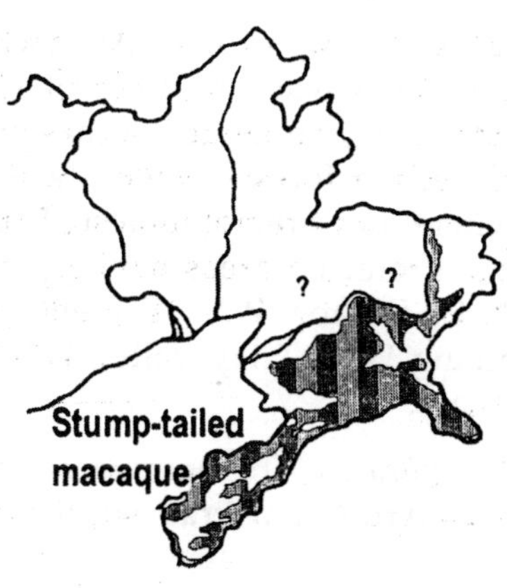

Remarks. Reviewed in detail by Fooden *et al.*, (1985). Geographical variation not clearly recognizable (Fooden, 1990). *M. speciosa* F. Cuvier, 1825 has been synonymised. IUCN: VU; WPA: Schedule II (I).

Subfamily COLOBINAE

Langurs

All the langurs found within India have been included in the Genus *Presbytis* (Ellerman & Morrison-Scott, 1951; Choudhury, 1997e). Groves (1989) put all the species except the Hanuman langur (*S. entellus*) into a separate genus *Trachypithecus* on the basis of the distinctive skull and the black pelage of the neonate (of *S. entellus*). Corbet & Hill (1992) included all the species in *Semnopithecus* because of close relationship of these groups and records of hybridization between *S. entellus* and *P. obscurus* (Hill, 1939) and between *S. entellus* and *P. johnii* (Hohmann, 1988). Unless general agreement is there, based upon further research and detailed reviews, except *S. entellus*, others have been included here in *Presbytis*. Even Corbet & Hill (1992) opined that 'there is no Indomalayan genus (of all primates) for which an adequate taxonomic revision exists'.

(87) **87. *Presbytis pileatus*** Capped langur
Semnopithecus pileatus Blyth, 1843: 174. TYPE-LOCALITY: unknown.

Local Names. *Honuman, Hanuman bandor* (A), *Bechar* (Adi), *Nuksu* (Aka), *Sibi bisar* (Apatani), *Hijua* (Bangni/Nishi, Bugun), *Pang-piyang* (Miji), *Ruksha* (Monpa), *Ragsha* (Monpa, Zemithang area), *Shra-la* (Singpho), *Rakang* (Tangsa), *Maijoh* (Wancho).

Distribution & Status. Found all over Arunachal Pradesh, W. of the Siang R. and E. of the Dibang R., from plains to up to 2800 m in the mountains. Strangely, no langur occurs in the tract between these two rivers. Chiefly a forest-dweller. Still common at many places, especially where they are not molested such as Tawang and W. Kameng districts. Protected areas having langurs are Mouling N.P., Namdapha N.P., Dibang W.S., Eaglenest W.S., Kane W.S., Itanagar W.S., Kamlang W.S., Taley Valley W.S., Mehao W.S., and Sessa Orchid Sanctuary.

Subspecies. 87a *P. p. pileatus*. The nominate race.
Hill forests in eastern Arunachal Pradesh, usually above 1000 m.
87b. *P. p. brahma*
P. brahma Wroughton, 1916a: 654. TYPE-LOCALITY: Seajuli, border area between Lakhimpur dist., Assam and Lower Subansiri dist.,

Capped langur

Arunachal Pradesh (originally recorded as Seajulia, Daffla Hills, N. Lakhimpur, Upper Assam).
Forests N. of the Brahmaputra R., in E. Kameng, Lower Subansiri, Papum Pare, Upper Subansiri, W. Siang, Upper Siang and E. Siang districts.
87c. *P. p. durga*
P. durga Wroughton, 1916b: 655. TYPE-LOCALITY: Cachar, Assam.
Occurs in the plains and foothills of eastern Arunachal Pradesh.
87d. *P. p. tenebricus* Hinton, 1923b: 81. Matunga R., N. Kamrup, Assam.
Found mainly in the western areas, in Tawang and W. Kameng districts.

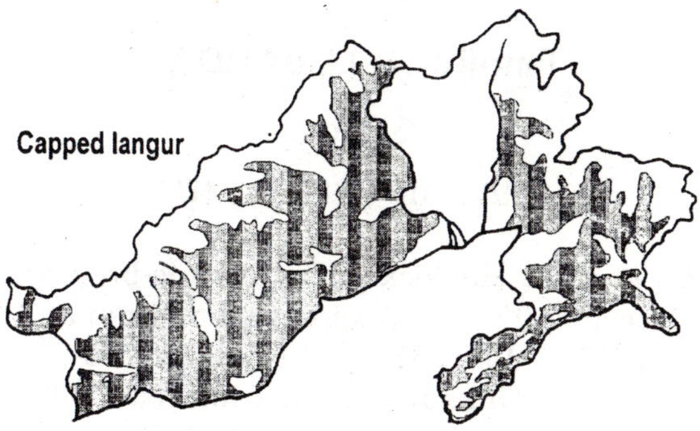

Remarks. The subspecific classification and their distribution need a detailed review as there are some seasonal variation in pelage colour and the ranges are unlikely to be strictly allopatric. Sympatric distribution means regular "hybridization" creating confusion in field identification. Specimens have been observed in the wild having characteristics of two or even three subspecies (Choudhury, 1997e).

Corbet & Hill (1992) mentioned of its occurrence up to 1000 m only but it has been recorded up to 2800 m elevation in Arunachal Pradesh (AUC).

There are occasional reports of the Hanuman or gray Langur *Semnopithecus entellus* from different parts of Arunachal Pradesh. On verification, all have been found to be cases of misidentification of the Capped langur. Known eastern limit of distribution of *S. entellus* is Buxa Tiger Reserve in northern West Bengal and adjacent areas of S.W. Bhutan (Choudhury, 1990d, 1997a). Corbet & Hill (1992) erroneously recorded Assam within its range while Tikader (1983) mentioned the Teesta R. in northern West Bengal as its eastern limit. Its record in Mouling N.P. (Chatterjee, 1989) was also misidentification of Capped langurs. Hence, there is no question of its presence in Arunachal Pradesh. Buxa is farther east of the Teesta R. Roonwal & Mohnot (1977) mentioned of a subspecies in N. Myanmar (*shanicus*) creating further confusion regarding the species' eastern limit (thus suggesting its occurrence in N.E. India also !). However, it is clear that no such race occurs in N. Myanmar (Burma).

Some tribes such as the Nishis use the pelt of the Capped langur as *dao*-cover (*Dao*= a cutting tool) while the Adis often use its skull as a pain-killer (they rub it against the affected part). CITES: Appendix I; IUCN: EN; WPA: Schedule I.

Family HYLOBATIDAE

Gibbons

Subfamily HYLOBATINAE

(89) **88 *Hylobates hoolock*** Hoolock gibbon, White-browed gibbon
Simia golok Bechstein, 1799: 70 (Suppressed by Opinion 1219 [1982]); *Simia hoolock* Harlan, 1831: 52, pl. 2 (Conserved by Opinion 1219 [1982]). TYPE-LOCALITY: Unknown (Bechstein); Garo Hills, Meghalaya (originally recorded as Assam), India (Harlan).

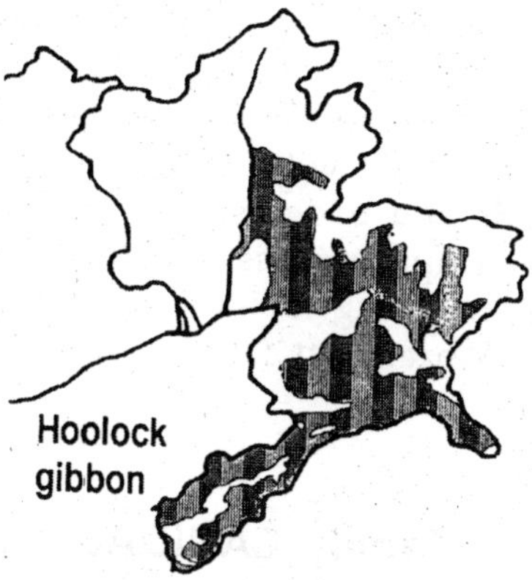

Local Names. *Holou bandor* (A), *Amepa* (Idu Mishmi), *Saka-huli, Chekkah* (Wancho).

Distribution & Status. Not uncommon in the forests S. of the Brahmaputra and E. of the Dibang Rivers. They do not occur N. of the Brahmaputra R. (Choudhury, 1987a, 1989f, 1991c). Found from plains to above 2000 m in the Mishmi Hills. Recorded in Dibang Valley, Lohit, Tirap and Changlang districts. Protected areas where the species is found are Namdapha N.P., Mehao W.S. and Kamlang W.S. Large population also occurs in Digaru, Kamlang, Manabum, Tengapani and Turung RFs (all in Lohit dist.). Some other notable areas (all reserved forests) are Diyun, Honkap, Miao, Namchik, Namdang, Namphuk, Pangsau, Rima (all in Changlang dist.), Borduria and Namsang (Tirap dist.).

Subspecies. 88a. *H. h. hoolock*. Nominate race.

Remarks. Not molested by the Mishmis, and hence, more abundant in Lohit and parts of Dibang Valley districts. CITES: Appendix I; IUCN: EN; WPA: Schedule I.

Order CARNIVORA

Carnivores

Dogs, cats, bears, civets, weasels, etc., are classified as Carnivora, the flesh-eating mammals or the beasts of prey. In size, they vary from small weasels to big cats like the tiger and the lion. Seven different families of carnivores are found in Arunachal Pradesh. They are Canidae (dogs and their allies), Ursidae (bears), Ailuridae (red panda), Mustelidae (weasels), Viverridae (civets), Herpestidae (mongooses) and Felidae (cats). Some families like Mustelidae and Viverridae contain animals with great external differences. For example, the weasels and badgers, both are placed in the same family but from their appearences it is difficult to believe. Some recent publications including reviews on carnivores are found in Flynn *et al.* (1988), Wozencraft (1989a, b), Gittelman (1989) and Choudhury (1997f).

Family CANIDAE

Dogs and Foxes

89. *Canis lupus* Wolf
C. lupus Linnaeus, 1758: 38. TYPE-LOCALITY: Sweden.

Distribution & Status. Very rare. Occasionally reported from near India-China border. Local reports from Mehao W.S. (A. Sen, *pc*) and Thingbu area of Tawang dist (Singh, 1991). The reports from Gaoligongshan in China (Ma *et al.*, 1994) also indicate possible occurrence in the state.

Subspecies. 89a. *C. l. chanco* Gray, 1863: 94. Tibetan wolf. TYPE-LOCALITY: Chinese Tartary.

Remarks. There are occasional reports of attack on domestic yaks. Reviewed by Mech (1974). CITES: Appendix I (India, Pakistan, Nepal and Bhutan), Appendix II (China); IUCN: LR (Lc); WPA: Schedule I.

(90) **90. *Canis aureus*** Golden jackal, Golden-backed jackal
C. aureus Linnaeus, 1758: 40. TYPE-LOCALITY: Lar Prov., Iran.

Local Names. *Hiyal* (A, Wancho), *Manru* (Adi).

Distribution & Status. Rare. Occurs in the countryside and wooded areas in towns and villages in the plains and foothills. Also in the fringe areas of forests. Frequently sighted in Santipur-Roing areas of Dibang Valley dist., Namsai-Sunpura areas of Lohit dist., Pasighat-Poba areas of E. Siang dist. and Banderdewa area of Papum Pare dist.

Subspecies. 90a. *C. a. indicus* Hodgson, 1833a: 237. TYPE-LOCALITY: Nepal.

Remarks. Population declined sharply due to persecution. WPA: Schedule II (II).

(91) **91. *Vulpes vulpes*** Red fox, Himalayan fox
Canis vulpes Linnaeus, 1758: 40. TYPE-LOCALITY: Sweden.

Local Name. *Hiyal* (A).

Distribution & Status. Found all over in the hills and mountains, usually from 1000 to up to 4000 m elevation. However, it is extremely rare and only occasionally seen.

Remarks. WPA: Schedule II (II).

(92) **92. *Vulpes bengalensis*** Bengal fox
Canis bengalensis Shaw, 1800: 330. TYPE-LOCALITY: Bengal.

Local Name. *Hiyal* (A).

Distribution & Status. Found in the hills and well-wooded countryside including vicinity of habitation in western Arunachal Pradesh. Rarer than the Jackal and Red fox and there is no recent sighting.

Remarks. IUCN: DD; WPA: Schedule II (II).

(93) **93. *Cuon alpinus*** Dhole, Indian wild dog, Red dog
Canis alpinus Pallas, 1811: 34. TYPE-LOCALITY: near Udskoi Ostrog, Uda R., Amur region, Russia. Conserved by Opinion 384 (1956).

Local Names. *Rang-kukur* (A), *Sipyang* (Adi), *Sipya* (Apatani), *Sachang* (Bangni/Nishi), *Shalu, Chai* (Bugun), *Bambu* (Idu Mishmi), *Phara* (Monpa), *Show* (Sherdukpen).

Distribution & Status. Found all over, in the forests from plains to mountains. Recorded up to 4000 m elevation. Not uncommon at suitable localities. Protected areas where the species has been recorded are Mouling N.P., Namdapha N.P., Eaglenest W.S., Itanagar W.S., Kamlang W.S., Kane W.S., Sessa Orchid Sanctuary, Pakhui W.S., Mehao W.S., and Taley Valley W.S. Also recorded in Amortola, Daporijo, Dibang, Doimara, Drupong, Namsang, Panir, Papum, Tengapani, and Turung RFs.

Remarks. It is not clear as to which subspecies occurs in Arunachal Pradesh. Two are likely to occur, *C. a. alpinus* (nominate race) or

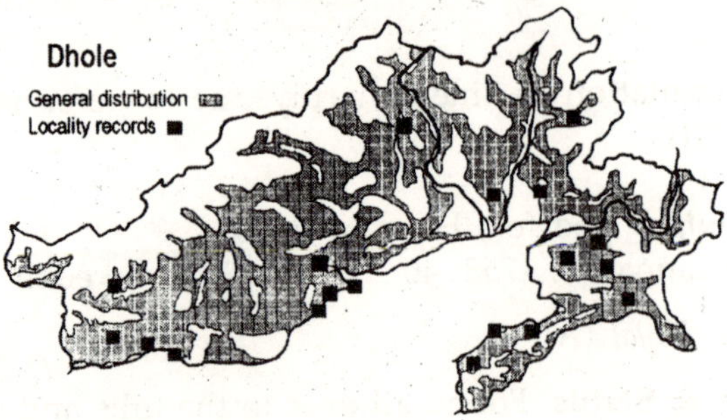

adustus Pocock, 1941: 156 (TYPE-LOCALITY: Upper Burma), and *primaevus* Hodgson, 1833a: 221 (TYPE-LOCALITY: Nepal). CITES: Appendix II; IUCN: VU; WPA: Schedule II (I). Attacks domestic stock including yaks, mithuns, sheep and horses. Often poisoned or shot by the villagers in retaliation.

Family URSIDAE

Bears

94. *Ursus arctos* Brown bear
Ursus arctos Linnaeus, 1758: 47. TYPE-LOCALITY: Sweden.

Distribution & Status. No specimen record so far. Reportedly very rare and confined to the trans-Himalaya and near India-China border. Probably occur in the extreme northern areas of Tawang, W. Kameng, and E. Kameng districts.

Subspecies. 94a. *U. a pruinosus* Blyth, 1854: 589. Tibetan blue bear. TYPE-LOCALITY: Lhasa, Tibet.

Remarks. CITES: Appendix II; WPA: Schedule I.

(94) **95. *Ursus thibetanus*** Himalayan black bear, Asiatic black bear
U. thibetanus Cuvier, G., 1823: 325. TYPE-LOCALITY: Sylhet, Bangladesh (originally recorded as 'Assam, India' as till 1947, Sylhet was a part of Assam).

Local Names. (All bears in general). *Bhâluk* (A), *Situm* (Adi), *Satum* (Bangni/Nishi), *Stûm* (Bugun), *Wâm* (Monpa), *Stûng* (Sherdukpen).

Distribution & Status. Found all over from foothills to mountains, up to 4000 m elevation. Also recorded from plains. Protected areas

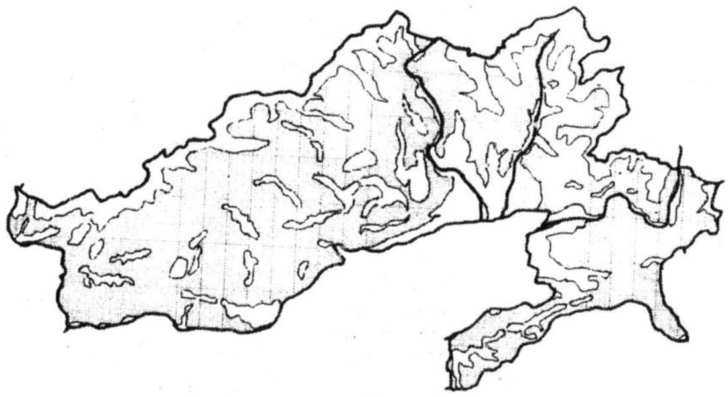

Himalayan black bear

where the species has been recorded are Mouling N.P., Namdapha N.P., Dibang W.S., Eaglenest W.S., Itanagar W.S., Kamlang W.S., Kane W.S., Mehao W.S., Pakhui W.S., Sessa Orchid Sanctuary and Taley Valley W.S.

Subspecies. 95a. *U. t. thibetanus.* Nominate race.

Remarks. So long included in the genus *Selenarctos* (Ellerman & Morrison-Scott, 1951; Heude, 1901), however, recent studies (Hoffmann in Wozencraft, 1989b; Corbet & Hill, 1992) put it in the genus *Ursus.* It is sympatric with *malayanus* in the south bank areas of the Brahmaputra R. and with *ursinus* in the foothills. Distribution in N.E. India incorrectly shown in Corbet & Hill (1992).

Once abundant all over, the species has become rare due to severe persecution by the poachers for its bile and gall bladder which are used in Oriental medicines. CITES: Appendix I; IUCN: VU; WPA: Schedule II (II).

(95) **96. *Ursus malayanus*** Sun bear, Malayan bear
U. malayanus Raffles, 1821: 254. TYPE-LOCALITY: Bencoolen, Sumatra, Indonesia. Conserved by Opinion 384 (1956).

Distribution & Status. Chiefly in the hill forests, S. of the Brahmaputra R. A few reports from the north bank which need confirmation. Mainly found in Tirap, Changlang and Lohit districts. Protected areas where the species has been recorded are Kamlang W.S. and Namdapha N.P. Patchily occurs all along the Patkai Range. Apparently rare and sighting records are few and far between.

Subspecies. 96a. *U.m. malayanus.* Nominate subspecies.

Remarks. Included in the genus *Helarctos* (Ellerman & Morrison-Scott, 1951; Horsfield, 1825). Considering close relationship with

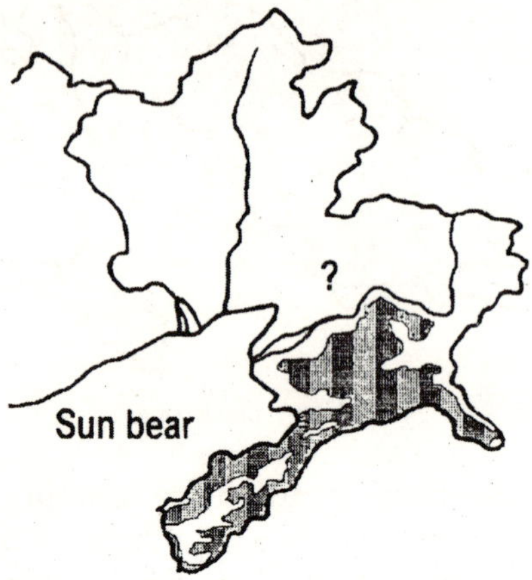

other bears and production of viable hybrids in captivity it has now been included in *Ursus* (Gray, 1972; Asakura, 1987; Corbet & Hill, 1992).

It is sympatric with *U. thibetanus* all over its range in Arunachal Pradesh as well as other parts of N.E. India. CITES: Appendix I; IUCN: DD; WPA: Schedule I.

97. (96) ***Ursus ursinus*** Sloth bear
Bradypus ursinus Shaw & Nodder, 1791: pls. 58–59. TYPE-LOCALITY: Patna, Bihar, India.

Local Names. *Bhâluk, Mâti-bhâluk* (A).

Distribution & Status. Rare in Arunachal Pradesh. Distributed in the forest and grassland in the plains and foothills. It is the only species of bear found in tall elephant-grass or wet savanna in addition to forests in the plains and foothills. It has become rarer. Protected areas having this species are Pakhui W.S. and D'Ering Memorial W.S.

Subspecies. 97a. *U. u. ursinus*. Nominate subspecies.

Remarks. Like the preceding two species, it has been included in the genus *Ursus* for similar reasons. Earlier considered a separate genus, *Melursus* (Meyer, 1793; Ellerman & Morrison-Scott, 1951). Distribution in N.E. India not shown on the map in Corbet & Hill (1992). CITES: Appendix III (India); IUCN: VU; WPA: Schedule I.

Family AILURIDAE

Red panda

98. *Ailurus fulgens* Red panda, Lesser panda
A. fulgens Cuvier, in Geoffroy & Cuvier, 1825: liv. 50. TYPE-LOCALITY: 'East Indies'. Conserved by Opinion 384 (1956).

Local Names. *Smamak, Smamum, Larai-niyam, Krackphu* (Bugun), *Aai-michinji* (Idu Mishmi), *Mamol* (Miji), *Thumnongkar, Thumdongkar* (Monpa), *Khumdongkar* (Monpa, Zemithang area).

Distribution & Status. The largest distribution range of the Red panda in India is in Arunachal Pradesh where it is found in the Himalaya and Mishmi Hills. The species is found in 11 of the 13 districts of the state, i.e., Tawang, W. Kameng, E. Kameng, Upper Subansiri, Lower Subansiri, Upper Siang, W. Siang, E. Siang, Dibang Valley, Lohit and Changlang. Presence suspected in Papum Pare dist.

Protected areas where it is found are Mouling N.P., Namdapha N.P., Dibang W.S., Eaglenest W.S., Kamlang W.S., Mehao W.S. and Sessa Orchid Sanctuary. Presence suspected in Pakhui W.S. and Taley Valley W.S. It has also been recorded in Dichu R.F., Delai proposed R.F., Kamlang R.F. (all in Lohit dist) and Nafra proposed Anchal R.F. (W. Kameng dist).

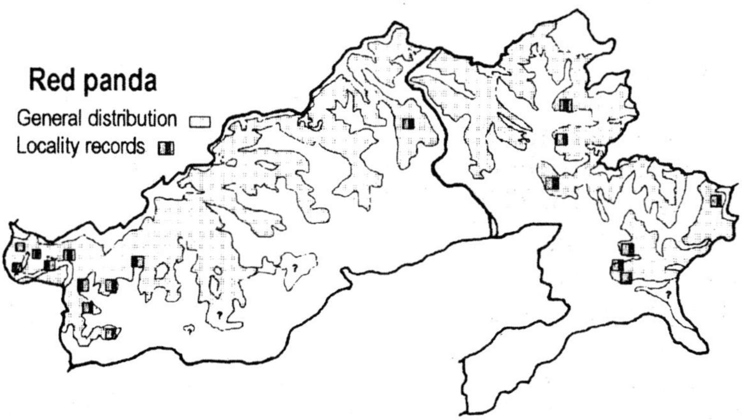

Subspecies. 98a. *A. f. fulgens.* Nominate subspecies.

Remarks. Reviewed by Roberts & Gittelman (1984), Glatston (1989) and Catton (1990). The recent status and range were reviewed and mapped by Choudhury (1997g, 2001). CITES: Appendix II; IUCN: EN; WPA: Schedule I.

Family MUSTELIDAE

Weasels & allies

Subfamily MUSTELINAE

Weasels and Martens

(97) **99. *Mustela kathiah*** Yellow-bellied weasel
M. (Putorices) kathiah Hodgson, 1835b: 702. TYPE-LOCALITY: Kachar, N. Nepal.

Distribution & Status. A high elevation species usually occurring above 1000 m elevation. Not uncommon all over Arunachal Pradesh.

Remarks. WPA: Schedule II (II).

100. *Mustela sibirica* Siberian weasel
M. sibirica Pallas, 1773: 701. TYPE-LOCALITY: Vorposten Tigerazkoi, near Ust-Kamenogorsk, W. Altai Mts., N.E. Kazakhstan.

Distribution & Status. Occurs in the mountains, usually above 2400 m elevation.

Remarks. IUCN: VU.

(98) **101. *Mustela strigidorsa*** Black-striped weasel
M. strigidorsa Hodgson in Gray, 1853: 191 (and Horsfield, 1855: 107). TYPE-LOCALITY: Sikkim, India.

Distribution & Status. Occurs in the hills and foothills all over, up to *c.* 2000 m elevation.

Remarks. IUCN: VU.

102. *Martes foina* Beech marten, Stone marten
Mustela foina Erxleben, 1777: 458. TYPE-LOCALITY: Germany.

Distribution & Status. Occurs above 1500 m in the Himalayas and N. Mishmi Hills.

Subspecies. 102a. *M. f. kozlovi* Ognev, 1931: 631. TYPE-LOCALITY: Kam, Mekong Valley, E. Tibet.

Remarks. WPA: Schedule II (II).

(99) **103.** ***Martes flavigula*** Yellow-throated marten
Mustela flavigula Boddaert, 1785: 88. TYPE-LOCALITY: Unknown, fixed as Nepal (Pocock, 1941).

Distribution & Status. Common, all over. Recorded occurring between 100 and 3000 m. Very common in some protected areas such as Namdapha N.P.

Subspecies. 103a. *M. f. flavigula*. Nominate subspecies.

Remarks. WPA: Schedule II (II).

M. flavigula

Subfamily MELINAE

Badgers

[***Meles meles*** Eurasian badger
Ursus meles Linnaeus, 1758: 48. TYPE-LOCALITY: Upsala, Sweden.

Distribution & Status. So far no specimen record but likely to occur near India-China border in Tawang, W. Kameng, E. Kameng, Lower Subansiri, Upper Subansiri, Upper Siang, Dibang Valley and Lohit districts. There are records from S.E. Tibet, not far from India-China border (Corbet & Hill, 1992). The records from N. Myanmar (Burma) (Tate, 1947), further indicate a possibility that badgers may occur in Arunachal Pradesh.

Subspecies. *M. m. leucurus*
Hodgson, 1847 c: 763. TYPE-LOCALITY: Lhasa, Tibet.]

M. meles

(101) **104. *Arctonyx collaris*** Hog-badger
A. collaris Cuvier, in Geoffroy & Cuvier, 1825: pt. 51, pl. TYPE-LOCALITY: Bhutan Duars, E. Himalayas.

Distribution & Status. Well distributed all over, in the forests as well as wooded countryside, from plains to mountains. The nominate subspecies occurs N. of the Brahmaputra R. and W. of the Siang R. while the subspecies *consul* is found S. of the Brahmaputra R. and E. of the Siang R., in eastern Arunachal Pradesh.

Subspecies. 104a. *A. c. collaris*. Nominate race.
104b. *A. c. consul* Pocock, 1940: 465. TYPE-LOCALITY: Thaundaung, near Toungoo, lower Burma (Myanmar), 4500 ft.

Remarks. WPA: Schedule I.

(102) **105. *Melogale personata*** Burmese ferret-badger, Large-toothed ferret-badger
M. personata Geoffroy, 1831: 137, pl. 5. TYPE-LOCALITY: near Rangoon (now Yangon), Burma (Myanmar).

Distribution & Status. Found all over in the forests. Specimen record near Roing, Dibang Valley dist (Chakraborty & Sen, 1991). Sightings very rare. The nominate race is mainly found S. of the Brahmaputra R., in eastern Arunachal Pradesh while the subspecies *nipalensis* in N. of the Brahmaputra R., in western and central Arunachal Pradesh.

Subspecies. 105a. *M. p. personata*.
105b. *M. p. nipalensis*
Gulo nipalensis Hodgson, 1836: 237. TYPE-LOCALITY: Nepal.

Remarks. WPA: Schedule II (I).

M. personata (top)
M. moschata (bottom)

(103) **106. *Melogale moschata*** Chinese ferret-badger, Small-toothed ferret-badger
Helictis moschata Gray, 1831: 94. TYPE-LOCALITY: Canton, Guangdong. S. China. Conserved by Opinion 384 (1956).

Distribution & Status. Found all over in the forests. Two specimens examined in Namdapha N.P. (Saha, 1985). Sightings very rare.

Subspecies. 106a. *M. m. millsi*
Helictis millsi Thomas, 1922b: 432. TYPE-LOCALITY: Mokokchung, Naga Hills (Nagaland; originally recorded as Assam), India.

Remarks. WPA: Schedule II (I).

Subfamily LUTRINAE

Otters

(104) **107. *Lutra lutra*** Common otter, Eurasian otter
Mustela lutra Linnaeus, 1758: 45. TYPE-LOCALITY: Upsala, Sweeden.

Local Names. (Generally for all otters). *Uud* (A), *Horam* (Adi), *Suja* (Aka), *Ama* (Bugun), *Sijam* (Miji), *Chilam, Ripchu* (Monpa).

Distribution & Status. Well distributed in the rivers, streams and other wetlands, often ascending above 3500 m in summer.

Subspecies. 107a. *L. l. monticolus*
L. monticolus Hodgson, 1839b: 320. TYPE-LOCALITY: Nepal.

Remarks. All species of otters have become very rare due to poaching for their skin, which is in great demand in Tibet for making garments, cap, etc. CITES: Appendix I. WPA: Schedule II (II). IUCN: VU.

(105) **108. *Lutrogale perspicillata*** Smooth Indian otter, Smooth-coated otter
Lutra perspicillata Geoffroy, I., 1826: 519. TYPE-LOCALITY: Sumatra, Indonesia.

Distribution & Status. Common in the plains and foothills affecting the wetlands.

Subspecies. 108a. *L. p. perspicillata.* Nominate subspecies.

Remarks. The genus *Lutrogale* was described by Gray (1865) and Corbet & Hill (1992) included *perspicillata* in this genus. However, for long it was included in *Lutra* (Ellerman & Morrison-Scott, 1951). CITES: Appendix II; IUCN: VU; WPA: Schedule II (II).

(106) **109. *Aonyx cinerea*** Oriental small-clawed otter, Clawless otter
Lutra cinerea Illiger, 1815: 90, 99. TYPE-LOCALITY: Batavia (Jakarta), Java, Indonesia.

Distribution & Status. Fairly common in the wetlands in the hills and plains. At Gandhigram, near Namdapha N.P., recorded at 1100 m elevation (Ghosh, 1987).

Subspecies. 109a. *A. c. concolor*
Amblonyx concolor Rafinesque, 1832: 62. TYPE-LOCALITY: Garo Hills, Meghalaya (originally recorded as Assam), India.

Remarks. CITES: Appendix II; IUCN: LR (nt); WPA: Schedule I.

Family VIVERRIDAE

Civets

Subfamily VIVERRINAE

Civets

110. (107) ***Viverra zibetha*** Large Indian civet
V. zibetha Linnaeus, 1758: 44. TYPE-LOCALITY: Bengal. Conserved by Opinion 384 (1956).

Large Indian civet

Local Name. *Gendera* (A).

Distribution & Status. Common all over in the forests and well-wooded countryside. The nominate subspecies occurs in W. Arunachal Pradesh, may be all over the N. bank of the Brahmaputra R. while *picta* in the S. bank areas, in E. Arunachal Pradesh.

Subspecies. 110a. *V. z. zibetha.* Nominate subspecies.
110b. *V. z. picta* Wroughton, 1915: 64. TYPE-LOCALITY: H'Kamti, Upper Chindwin R., N. Burma (Myanmar), 500 ft.

Remarks. WPA: Schedule II (II).

(108) **111. *Viverricula indica*** Small Indian civet
Viverra indica Desmarest, 1817: 170. TYPE-LOCALITY: India.

Local Names. *Johamol, Hapa* (A).

Distribution & Status. Very common all over including human habitations in towns and villages. A known killer of domestic fowl.

Subspecies. 111a. *V. i. baptistae* Pocock, 1933a: 643. TYPE-LOCALITY: Hasimara, Jalpaiguri dist (north Bengal *Duars*), West Bengal, India (originally recorded as Bhutan *Duars*).

Remarks. WPA: Schedule II (II).

(109) **112. *Prionodon pardicolor*** Spotted linsang
P. pardicotor[*sic*] Hodgson, 1841c: 57. TYPE-LOCALITY: Not known.

Distribution & Status. Found in the forests, especially in the foot-hills and hills. Very rare. Some recent records are, skin and skull in Siang area (Katti *et al.*, 1990), two lone animals between Roing and Mayodia in Mehao W.S. (Chakraborty & Sen, 1991), reports from Mouling N.P. (Singh *et al.*, 1996), one in February, 1999 near Pakhui W.S. (near Assam, Arunachal Pradesh border in Nameri N.P.; P. Saikia *pc*). One caught in Itanagar town is now in the local zoo.

Remarks. CITES: Appendix I; WPA: Schedule I.

Spotted linsang

Subfamily PARADOXURINAE

Palm civets

(110) **113. *Paradoxurus hermaphroditus*** Common palm civet, Toddy cat
Viverra hermaphrodita Pallas, in Schreber, 1777: 426. TYPE-LOCALITY: ? India. Conserved by Opinion 384 (1956).

Local Name. *Siran* (Adi).

Distribution & Status. Common in the forests, countryside and well-wooded towns. Often haunts dwelling houses at night in semi-urban and village areas.

Subspecies. 113a. *P. h. pallasii*
P. pallasii Gray, 1832: 67. TYPE-LOCALITY: India.

Remarks. Subspecific classification may be treated as tentative. WPA: Schedule II (II).

(111) **114. *Paguma larvata*** Masked palm civet, Himalayan palm civet
Gulo larvatus Hamilton-Smith, 1827: 281, pl. TYPE-LOCALITY: Unknown, probably S. China.

Distribution & Status. Common all over especially in the foothills and hills. Affects forest.

Subspecies. 114a. *P. l. neglecta* Pocock, 1934: 334. TYPE-LOCALITY: Mokokchung, Nagaland (originally recorded as Assam), India, 4500 ft.

Remarks. WPA: Schedule II (II).

(112) **115. *Arctictis binturong*** Binturong, Bear-cat
Viverra? binturong Raffles, 1821: 253. TYPE-LOCALITY: Malacca, Malaysia. Conserved by Opinion 384 (1956).

Local Name. *Yong* (A).

Distribution & Status. Found all over in the forested hills and foothills. Becoming rarer due to habitat loss. Protected areas where the species is found or has been recorded are Mouling N.P., Namdapha N.P., Eaglenest W.S., Itanagar W.S., Kamlang W.S., Kane W.S., Mehao W.S., Pakhui W.S., Sessa Orchid Sanctuary and Taley Valley W.S. There are also records from Dibang, and Panir RFs.

Subspecies. 115a. *A. b. albifrons*
Paradoxurus albifrons Cuvier, F., 1822: 44, 48. TYPE-LOCALITY: Bhutan.

Remarks. WPA: Schedule I.

(113) **116. *Arctogalidia trivirgata*** Small-toothed palm civet
Paradoxurus trivirgatus Gray, 1832: 68. TYPE-LOCALITY: Unknown. Conserved by Opinion 384 (1956).

Distribution & Status. Found in the forests, especially in the hills and foothills, south of the Brahmaputra R., in eastern Arunachal Pradesh. Very rare.

Subspecies. 116a. *A. t. millsi*
Arctogalidia millsi Wroughton, 1921a: 600. TYPE-LOCALITY: Mokokchung, Nagaland (originally recorded as Assam), India, 5000 ft.

Remarks. WPA: Schedule II (II).

Family HERPESTIDAE

Mongooses

(114) **117. *Herpestes javanicus*** Small Asian mongoose, Small Indian mongoose
Ichneumon javanicus Geoffroy, E. 1818: 138. TYPE-LOCALITY: W. Java, Indonesia.

Local Name. *Newul* (A, all mongooses).

Distribution & Status. Very common all over including towns and villages. Mainly affects plains and foothills.

Subspecies. 117a. *H. j. auropunctatus*
Mangusta auropunctata Hodgson, 1836: 235. TYPE-LOCALITY: Nepal.

Remarks. Chasen (1940) and Ellerman & Morrison-Scott (1951) treated *auropunctatus* and *javanicus* as two distinct species. However, because of insignificant difference they are combined by Pocock (1941) and Lekagul & McNeely (1977). WPA: Schedule IV.

(115) **118.** ***Herpestes edwardsii*** Indian grey mongoose
Ichneumon edwardsii Geoffroy, E., 1818: 139. TYPE-LOCALITY: 'East Indies', designated as Madras, India (Pocock, 1933b).

Distribution & Status. Mainly found in western Arunachal Pradesh. Also elsewhere, recorded near Mehao W.S. (Chakraborty & Sen, 1991). Not uncommon. Mainly affects plains and foothills, occasionally near human habitations.

Subspecies. 118a. *H. e. nyula* Hodgson, 1836a: 235. TYPE-LOCALITY: Nepal.

Remarks. Subspecific variations are slight and may need a detailed revision. WPA: Schedule IV.

(116) **119.** ***Herpestes urva*** Crab-eating mongoose
Gulo urva Hodgson, 1836: 238. TYPE-LOCALITY: Nepal.

Distribution & Status. Found all over, especially in the wetlands and forest streams. Rarer than the other two species. Unlike others (which are mostly met with singly), this species is usually seen in twos or more.

Remarks. The Stripe-necked mongoose *H. vitticollis* recorded in Dichu R.F. (Singh *et al.*, 1995) actually belongs to this species. Former is confined to S. India and Sri Lanka. WPA: Schedule IV.

Crab-eating mongoose

Family FELIDAE

Cats

(117) **120. *Felis chaus*** Jungle cat
F. chaus Gueldenstaedt, 1776: 483. TYPE-LOCALITY: Terek R., N. of Caucasus.

Local Names. *Bon-mekuri, Bonbonda* (A), *Tassi* (Adi), *Aschangu* (Idu Mishmi, lesser cats in general), *Susu-nambu* (Monpa).

Distribution & Status. Common all over the state. It is the most abundant of the small felids found in the area. Affects forest, forest-edge, plantations and vicinity of human habitation where it is a known killer of domestic fowl.

The subspecies *affinis* is found in the N. bank of the Brahmaputra R. while *fulvidina* in the S. bank areas, especially in E. Arunachal Pradesh.

Subspecies. 120a. *F. c. affinis*
F. affinis Gray, 1830 (in 1830–35): pl. 3. TYPE-LOCALITY: Gangotri, Tehri Garhwal, Uttar Pradesh, India.
120b. *F. c. fulvidina*
F. affinis fulvidina Thomas, 1929: 834. TYPE-LOCALITY: Kampong Tomb, Annam, Vietnam.

Remarks. The subspecific classification is mainly based upon minor differences in size and length of the pelage. Hence, these may be treated as tentative. WPA: Schedule II (II).

(118) **121. *Felis bengalensis*** Leopard cat
F. bengalensis Kerr, 1792: 151. TYPE-LOCALITY: S. Bengal, India.

Local Names. *Lota-mekuri bagh* (A), *Hole* (Adi), *Sigi* (Bugun), *Susu-nambu* (Monpa).

Distribution & Status. Well distributed in the forests, from plains to hills. Still fairly common and alongwith *F. chaus,* is among the most abundant small felids in Arunachal Pradesh. Found in all the protected areas of the State.

Subspecies. 121a. *F. b. bengalensis.* Nominate subspecies. Found all over.
121b. *F. b. horsfieldii*
F. horsfieldii Gray, 1842: 260. TYPE-LOCALITY: Bhutan. Probably in western Arunachal Pradesh.

Remarks. Included in the genus *Prionailurus* (Severtzov, 1858; Corbet & Hill, 1992) mainly on the basis of pattern of stripes and colouration rather than cranial, dental or other more concrete characteristics. The subspecific classification and their distribution need a detailed review. CITES: Appendix I /II; WPA: Schedule I.

(119) **122. *Felis viverrinus*** Fishing cat
F. viverrinus Bennett, 1833: 68. TYPE-LOCALITY: India, probably the Malabar coast.

Local Name. *Meseka* ? (A).

Distribution & Status. Distributed all over Arunachal Pradesh in well-watered localities. Rare. Protected areas having the species are Namdapha N.P., Eaglenest W.S., Itanagar W.S., Kamlang W.S., Mehao W.S., Pakhui W.S., Sessa Orchid Sanctuary and ? Taley Valley W.S.

Remarks. Considered as *Felis* instead of *Prionailurus* for reasons mentioned in *bengalensis*. IUCN: VU; WPA: Schedule I.

(120) **123. *Felis temminckii*** Golden cat
F. temminckii Vigors & Horsfield, 1827: 451. TYPE-LOCALITY: Sumatra, Indonesia.

Local Name. *Zik* (Monpa).

Distribution & Status. Found in the forests all over. Very rare and sight records are few. Definite records from Lower Subansiri, E. Kameng and Papum Pare districts. In the first named area, the local Hill Miris occasionally snare it. One such animal was photographed by a group of anglers at Gaimukh on the banks of the Subansiri R. in November, 1997 (Atul Borgohain, *pc*). There is also a sight record at Di-ring in Papum Pare dist in 1968.

Remarks. Included in a separate genus *Catopuma* (Severtzov, 1858; Corbet & Hill, 1992) on the basis of minor colour patterns and shades. Distribution in India not correctly shown in Corbet & Hill (1992). CITES: Appendix I; IUCN: VU; WPA: Schedule I.

124. (121) ***Felis marmorata*** Marbled cat
F. marmorata Martin, 1837: 108. TYPE-LOCALITY: Sumatra, Indonesia (Robinson & Kloss, 1919: 261).

Local Name. *Simnyo-nyeling* (Adi).

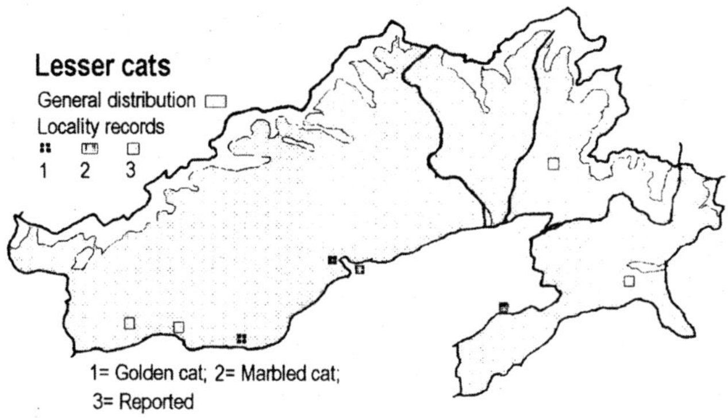

Distribution & Status. Forests in the hills and foothills all over. Rare. Recent records, one skin from Mehao W.S. (Chakraborty & Sen, 1991), another skin from degraded evergreen forest in Subansiri R.F., Dhemaji dist of Assam in 1990. Subansiri R.F. is on the Assam-Arunachal Pradesh border with contiguous habitat. The Subansiri specimen also happened to be the largest known in the world with a head-and-body length of 65 cm. (Choudhury, 1996f).

Remarks. Included in the genus *Pardofelis* by Severtzov (1858) and Corbet & Hill (1992). Latter also clubbed the Marbled cat and the Clouded leopard in the same genus which perhaps needs further justification as except the pattern of their coat, there is little similarity to warrant inclusion in the same genus. Moreover, the cranial and dental characteristics of *nebulosa* are significantly different from all other cats.

The subspecific classification, especially of the mainland animals needs a fresh review. Ellerman & Morrison-Scott (1951) suggests that the race occurs in Assam and adjacent areas is *F. m. charltonii* Gray, 1846: 211 (TYPE-LOCALITY: Darjeeling, West Bengal, India).

Distribution in India by Corbet & Hill (1992) incorrectly shown. CITES: Appendix I; IUCN: VU; WPA: Schedule I.

(122) **125. *Neofelis nebulosa*** Clouded leopard
Felis nebulosa Griffith, 1821: 37. TYPE-LOCALITY: Canton, S. China.

Local Names. *Godha-futuki bagh* (A), *Karbok* (Bangni / Nishi), *Panchat* (Miji), *Gungser, Sagretpoh* (Monpa).

Distribution & Status. In the forested hills, foothills and edge of the hills all over Arunachal Pradesh. Very rare. Recent records

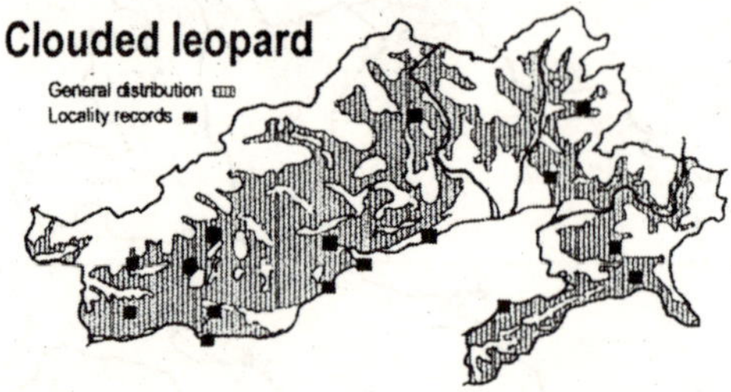

including skins and skulls suggest thin but widespread distribution. Recorded in Mouling N.P., Namdapha N.P., Kamlang W.S. (Choudhury, 1996h), Mehao W.S., Pakhui W.S., near Panir R.F. and Taley Valley W.S. (Dey, 1995), and near Seijosa (sighted inside Assam, Pratap Singh, *pc*). Also reported from Dibang W.S., Eaglenest W.S., Itanagar W.S., and Sessa Orchid Sanctuary. There is also a specimen record from Assam-Arunachal Pradesh border in W. Siang dist (Choudhury, 1993a).

Subspecies. 125a. *N. n. macroselloides*
Felis macroselloides Hodgson in Gray, 1853: 192 (= *F. macrosceloides* in pl. 38). TYPE-LOCALITY: Nepal.

Remarks. Included in the genus *Pardofelis* by Corbet & Hill (1992) (also see remarks in *marmorata*). CITES: Appendix I; IUCN: VU; WPA: Schedule I.

(123) **126. *Panthera pardus*** Leopard, Panther
Felis pardus Linnaeus, 1758: 41. TYPE-LOCALITY: Egypt. Conserved by Opinion 1368 (1985).

Local Names. *Nahorfutuki bagh* (A), *Ghoong* (A, Black panther), *Thakkar* (Adi), *Hoge-takke* (Apatani), *Kargong* (Bangni/Nishi), *Ichi* (Idu Mishmi), *Bartak, Gungtak* (Monpa), *Chanu* (Wancho).

Distribution & Status. Well distributed in the forests. Still fairly common. It is also found in most of the protected areas. Recorded at 4100 m elevation at Nagula, Tawang dist.

Subspecies. 126a. *P. p. fusca*
Felis fusca Meyer, 1794: 394. TYPE-LOCALITY: Bengal, India.

Remarks. CITES: Appendix I; WPA: Schedule I.

(124) **127.** ***Panthera tigris*** Tiger, Indian tiger, Bengal tiger
Felis tigris Linnaeus, 1758: 41. TYPE-LOCALITY: Bengal, India.

Local Names. *Bãgh, Dhekiapotia bãgh* (A), *Sîmyo* (Adi), *Kheche* (Aka), *Pâté* (Apatani), *Senio* (Bangni/Nishi), *Mûchua* (Bugun), *Ama* (Idu Mishmi), *Tîngran* (Miji), *Bushu* (Monpa), *Bu-ata* (Monpa, Zemithang area), *Fooh* (Sherdukpen), *Chãnu* (Wancho).

Distribution & Status. Widespread in the forests and grassland, from floodplains to the mountains. Not uncommon at suitable localities. Protected areas with large population (>50) are Namdapha N.P. and Pakhui W.S. The protected areas having >10 tigers are Mouling N.P., D'Ering Memorial W.S., Dibang W.S., Eaglenest W.S., Itanagar W.S., Kamlang W.S., Mehao W.S., Sessa Orchid Sanctuary and Taley Valley W.S. Also found in Kane W.S.

Subspecies. 127a. *P. t. tigris* Linnaeus, 1758. Bengal tiger. Nominate subspecies.

Remarks. Also often called the Royal Bengal tiger. There is a recent spurt in poaching all over its range for its bone which is used in Chinese medicine. CITES: Appendix I; IUCN: EN; WPA: Schedule I.

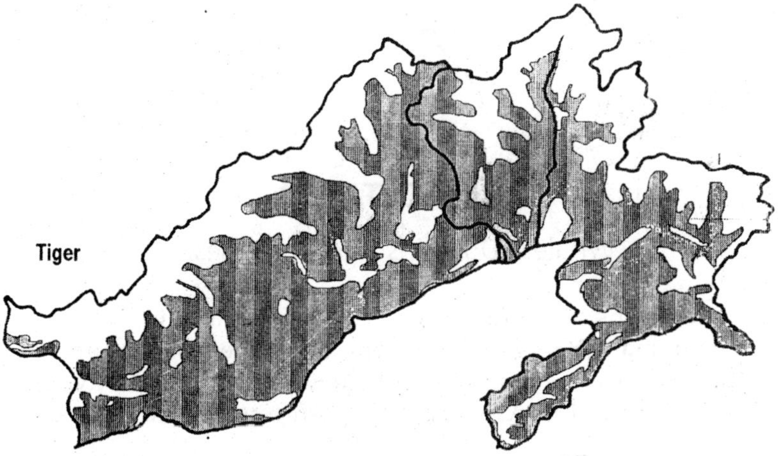

128. *Uncia uncia* Snow leopard, Ounce
Felis uncia Schreber, 1776: 100 (1776), 386, 586 (1777). TYPE-LOCALITY: Unknown.

Local Name. *Yuodi simyo* (Adi).

Distribution & Status. Very rare. Found in the Great Himalaya, trans-Himalaya and the highest parts of Mishmi Hills and Dapha Bum. Past record from Se-la (Gee, 1964), on the border of present Tawang and W. Kameng districts. Local reports from the higher areas, usually above 4000 m, in E. Kameng, Upper Subansiri, Upper Siang, Dibang Valley, Lohit and Changlang districts. Protected areas from where it has been reported (however, no specimen record so far) are Namdapha N.P., Mouling N.P., Dibang W.S. and Mehao W.S. (only in winter). In the last named site, pugmarks recorded on snow at 2560–2880 m during winter (Chakraborty & Sen, 1991). Also reported from Dichu R.F. in Lohit dist.

Remarks. Often put in a separate genus *Uncia* because of some craniological, morphological and ethological characteristics (Heptner & Sludskii, 1992). CITES: Appendix I; IUCN: EN; WPA: Schedule I.

Order CETACEA

Whales, Dolphins and Porpoises

Whales, dolphins and porpoises are classified as Cetacea, or the marine mammals. Regarded as among the earliest of the surviving mammals, the Cetaceans have developed a fish-like body. Only one family is found in Arunachal Pradesh represented by a single species.

Suborder ODONTOCETI

Family PLATANISTIDAE

River dolphins

(125) **129. *Platanista gangetica*** Gangetic dolphin, Susu
Delphinus gangeticus Roxburgh, 1801: 171. TYPE-LOCALITY: Ganges Delta, near Calcutta, West Bengal, India. Conserved by Opinion 1565 (1989).

Local Name. *Sihu* (A).

Distribution & Status. Very rare and occasional in Arunachal Pradesh. Found only in the lower reaches of the Siang, Dibang, Lohit, Subansiri, Noa-Dihing and Burhi-Dihing rivers. Mostly seen during monsoon.

Remarks. It has been reviewed by Reeves & Brownell (1989). Population declined sharply due to poaching for oil and also accidental trapping in fishing nets in the main Brahmaputra R. in Assam. CITES: Appendix I; IUCN: EN; WPA: Schedule I.

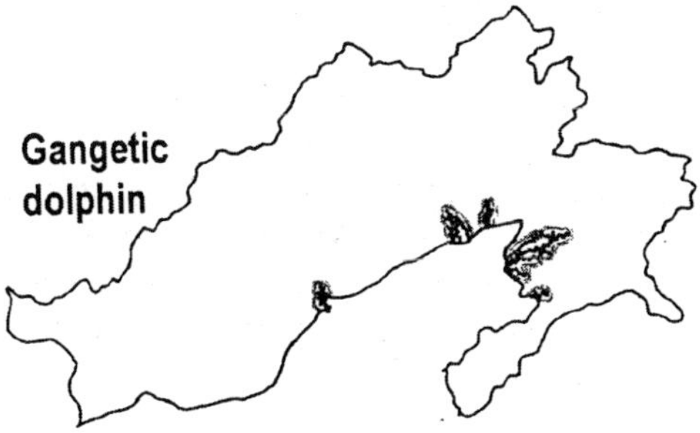

Order PROBOSCIDEA

Elephants

The elephants of Asia and Africa comprise the order Proboscidea, which has only two genus, *Loxodonta* and *Elephas*. Only one genus (*Elephas*) occurs in Assam as well as other parts of Asia. The name Proboscidea is derived from the proboscis or the trunk of the elephant.

Family ELEPHANTIDAE

Elephants

(126) **130.** ***Elephas maximus*** Asian elephant, Indian elephant
E. maximus Linnaeus, 1758: 33. TYPE-LOCALITY: Sri Lanka.

Local Names. *Haathi* (A), *Gonesh* (A, especially one-tusked male), *Mokhna* (A, tuskless male), *Sot* (Adi), *Sété* (Apatani), *Nathong* (Bugun), *Ãta* (Idu Mishmi), *Hãti* (Miji), *Stong* (Sherdukpen), *Lûak* (Wancho).

Distribution & Status. Common in the forests and grasslands. Mainly occurs in the foothills, edge of the hills and the plains along the main rivers. However, occasionally move up in the mountains. The highest elevation haunted by elephants is Piri La at 3200 m in Eaglenest W.S. (recorded in 1997). Occurs in two large discrete populations totalling more than 2000 (range: 1600–2700; 2098 counted in 1993 census). One population ranges from W. Kameng through E. Kameng, Lower Subansiri, Papum Pare, W. Siang, E. Siang to the S.W. corner of Dibang Valley districts (numbers fluctuate between 900 and 1700; 1218 counted in 1993). The other population ranges from S.W. part of Dibang Valley to Tirap through Lohit and Changlang districts (range: 700–1000 elephants; 880 counted in 1993).

The two populations have been separated by a gap in Dibang Valley dist (Choudhury, 1995d). Protected areas having large population are Namdapha N.P. and Pakhui W.S. Other protected areas having elephants are D'Ering Memorial W.S., Eaglenest W.S., Itanagar W.S., Mehao W.S., Sessa Orchid Sanctuary and Kane W.S. Reserved forests having sizeable populations are Amortola, Dibang,

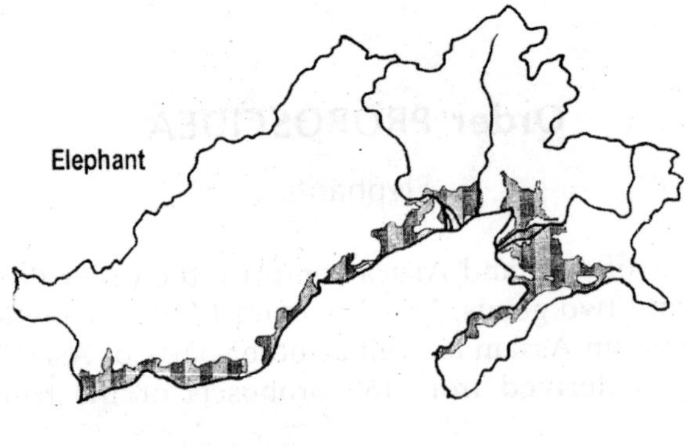

Diyun, Doimara, Doimukh (proposed), Drupong, Jiadhal (proposed) Manabum, Mebo, Miao, Namsang, Panir, Papum, Remi, Tengapani, and Turung.

Subspecies. 130a. *E. m. bengalensis*
Blainville, 1845: 353, pl. iii. TYPE-LOCALITY: Bengal.

Remarks. Distribution in N.E. India not correctly shown on the maps in Corbet & Hill (1992) and Sukumar (1989). Poaching for ivory and also meat has threatened the species in some areas. Subspecific variations are insignificant. CITES: Appendix I; IUCN: EN; WPA: Schedule I.

Order PERISSODACTYLA

Odd-toed ungulates

The order Perissodactyla or the odd-toed ungulates consists of three very distinct families, the rhinoceroses (Rhinocerotidae), horses (Equidae) and the tapirs (Tapiridae). The ungulates or hoofed animals are divided into two orders, depending upon the arrangement of their toes. In the odd-toed ungulates, the third or middle toe of the foot is the most prominent. The rhinoceroses have also distinctive 'horns'. The evolution of perissodactyls was reviewed by Prothero & Schoch (1989).

Family RHINOCEROTIDAE

Rhinoceroses

(127) **131. *Rhinoceros unicornis*** Indian rhinoceros, Greater one-horned rhinoceros
R. unicornis Linnaeus, 1758: 56. TYPE-LOCALITY: ? Assam, India.

Local Names. *Gorh* (A), *Charak* (Adi, Mising).

Distribution & Status. No resident population but almost every year, a few animals stray into Arunachal Pradesh, mostly from Kaziranga N.P. of Assam. Some recent records are from Pakhui W.S., Papum R.F., Drupong R.F. and Panir R.F. (Choudhury, 1997h).

Remarks. Earlier, there were small permanent populations in Sonai-Rupai W.S. and Lakhimpur dist of Assam, both close to Arunachal Pradesh. Also known as the Indian one-horned or Great Indian

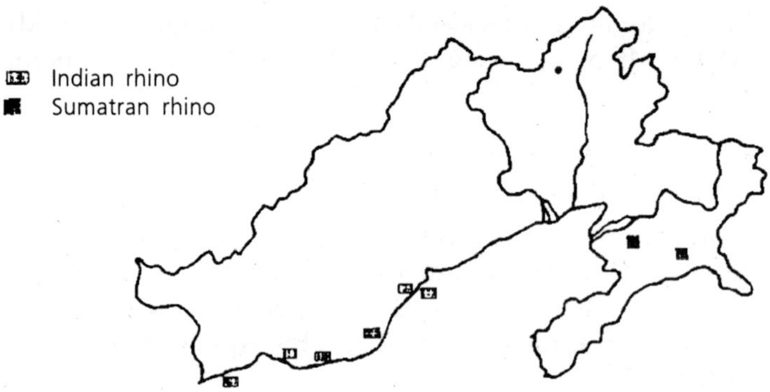

one-horned rhinoceros. CITES: Appendix I; IUCN: EN; WPA: Schedule I.

(129) **132.** ***Dicerorhinus sumatrensis*** Sumatran rhinoceros, Asian two-horned rhinoceros

Rhinoceros sumatrensis Fischer, 1814: 301. TYPE-LOCALITY: Bencoolen dist., S. Sumatra, Indonesia. Conserved by Opinion 1080 (1977).

Distribution & Status. Extinct in the last century. However, stragglers were reported in the first few decades of the present century. There were two definite records (Rookmaker, 1980), at Nam Tsai, *c.* 27°30′ N., 97°00′ E. in 1895 (Henri, 1898), and in Noa-Dihing R., *c.* 27°20′ N., 96°20′ E. in about 1953 (Shebbeare, 1953), former probably in present Lohit dist while latter in Changlang dist, and were in or around Namdapha N.P. In the adjacent areas of Myanmar (Burma), there are reports of continued occurrence from Hukawng Valley (Choudhury, 1997b).

Subspecies. 132a. *D. s. lasiotis*
Rhinoceros lasiotis Buckland, 1872: 89. TYPE-LOCALITY: Chittagong, E. Bengal (now Bangladesh).

Remarks. Included in the genus *Didermocerus* (Brookes, 1828; Ellerman & Morrison-Scott, 1951). Although believed to have become extinct in the Indian subcontinent in the 19th century, one was killed in 1967 near Cox's Bazar in the Chittagong dist of Bangladesh (Cubitt & Mountfort, 1985) and stragglers are still encountered in Nagaland and Manipur, especially near the Indo-Myanmarese border (Choudhury, 1997b). CITES: Appendix I; IUCN: CR.

Order ARTIODACTYLA

Even-toed ungulates

The even-toed ungulates are classified as order Artiodactyla. The pigs, deer, antelopes, oxen, goats and sheep comprise this order. The feet of these ungulates are designed and also well adapted for continuous travel for long distances. Three families represent this order in Assam, these are Suidae (pigs), Bovidae (oxen and goat-antelopes) and Cervidae (deer). The Bovidae differs from the Cervidae in having permanent horns, with a bony core and a hollow outer sheath covering it. The deer have solid horns called antlers which are shed periodically.

Family SUIDAE

Pigs

(131) **133.** ***Sus scrofa*** Wild pig, Wild boar
S. scrofa Linnaeus, 1758: 49. TYPE-LOCALITY: Germany. Conserved by Opinion 75 (1922).

Local Names. *Bonoria gãhori, Bonborah* (A), *Shira* (Adi), *Sre* (Apatani), *Dicheng* (Bugun), *Amé* (Idu Mishmi), *Risha* (Monpa), *Pengpha* (Monpa, Zemithang area), *Skan* (Sherdukpen), *Meila* (Wancho).

Distribution & Status. Common all over Arunachal Pradesh affecting forests and grasslands from plains to above 3000 m in the mountains. Occurs in most of the protected areas and still abundant at suitable places.

Subspecies. 133a. *S. s. cristatus*
S. cristatus Wagner, 1839: 435 (misprinted as 535). TYPE-LOCALITY: near Calcutta, West Bengal, India (Groves, 1981).

Remarks. This species is the ancestor of the domestic pig. WPA: Schedule III.

(132) **134.** ***Sus salvanius*** Pygmy hog, Pigmy hog
Porcula salvania Hodgson, 1847a: 423, pl. 12, 13. TYPE-LOCALITY: Sikkim Terai (now in northern West Bengal), India.

Local Names. *Nal gâhori, Tâkori borah* (A).

Distribution & Status. No specific record so far but probably existed in the grasslands along the Jia-Bhoreli, Bor-Dikorai, Nameri,

Papum, Buroi and Borgang rivers as in the adjacent areas of Assam, it was found. Extremely rare and sightings in the wild very difficult.

Remarks. A very restricted range species with historic range confined to the *terai* grassland from Nepal to Assam. Vanished from most of its former range with surviving population confined to two pockets of Assam, in Manas N.P. and Bornadi W.S. A captive breeding centre has started functioning near Guwahati in 1996 with a few wild-caught animals from Manas N.P. The grassy patches in Papum, and Drupong RFs may be worth surveying for any remnant population. CITES: Appendix I; IUCN: CR; WPA: Schedule I.

Family CERVIDAE

Deer

Subfamily MOSCHINAE

135. *Moschus moschiferus* Himalayan musk deer
M. moschiferus Linnaeus, 1758: 66. TYPE-LOCALITY: 'Tartary, approaching China'.

Local Names. *Kosturi horin* (A), *Hodung, Sibuei, Sikung* (Adi), *Garawa, Loh* (Monpa), *Lawa* (Monpa, Zemithang area).

Distribution & Status. Once widespread and common all over the mountains, Himalaya, Mishmi Hills and Dapha Bum but now very rare although the general range of distribution remains more or less same. Usually found above 2800 m elevation in Tawang, W. Kameng, E. Kameng, Upper Subansiri, Lower Subansiri, Upper Siang, W. Siang, Dibang Valley, Lohit and Changlang districts.

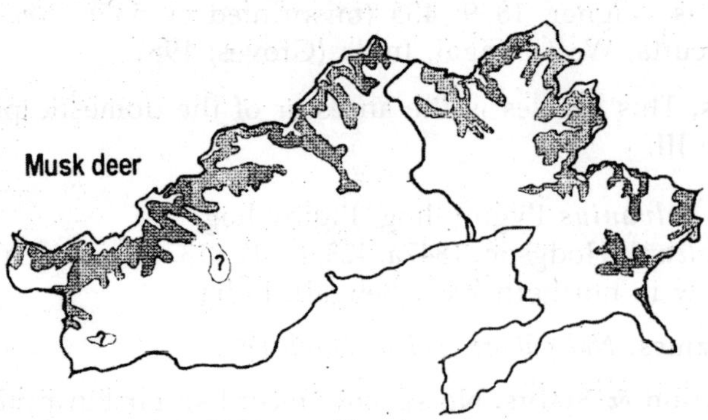

Protected areas having the species are Mouling N.P., Namdapha N.P., Dibang W.S., ? Eaglenest W.S., and Mehao W.S. Also in Dichu R.F., Lohit dist.

Remarks. Included in a separate family, Moschidae, by Groves & Grubb (1987) and Corbet & Hill (1992). The classification of the genus *Moschus* is still uncertain to a great extent. Ellerman & Morrison-Scott (1951) considered all forms as conspecific while Groves *et al.* (1995) proposed six species. Of the six proposed species, at least two, *M. fuscus* Li, 1981 (in eastern Arunachal Pradesh), and *M. chrysogaster* Hodgson, 1839a (in western Arunachal Pradesh) occurs in the state. Groves *et al.* (1995), however, opined that 'complete solution to the problem of Musk deer taxonomy still somewhat elusive'. The general consensus is that at least three are clearly recognisable with probable more, *M. moschiferus* in the Himalayas, *M. sibiricus* in Palaeacrtic and *M. berezovskii* in south and central China. Persecuted by poachers for its musk pod all over its range. CITES: Appendix I; IUCN: VU (*moschiferus* syn. *sibiricus*), LR (nt) (*fuscus, chrysogaster*); WPA: Schedule I.

Subfamily CERVINAE

(133) **136. *Cervus duvauceli*** Swamp deer, Barasingha
C. duvauceli Cuvier, G., 1823: 505. TYPE-LOCALITY: not recorded, presumably N. India.

Local Names. *Dal horina, Bhelengi pohu* (A).

Distribution & Status. No recent record. Past occurrence reported from the elephant-grass jungles along the Siang, Dibang and Lohit rivers in E. Siang, Dibang Valley and Lohit districts. Probably locally extinct.

Remarks. Groves (1982) reviewed the subspecific variation and suggested a new race *C.d. ranjitsinhi* for the animals from Assam. However, specimens examined by Groves were very few and significant individual variation have been observed in the field as well as in the preserved antlers. Therefore, till a further detailed review is done on the basis of more specimens, the animals found in N.E. India are treated here as *C.d. duvauceli* (nominate race). CITES: Appendix I; IUCN: VU (ssp. *duvauceli*), CR (ssp. *ranjitsinhi*); WPA: Schedule I.

(134) **137. *Cervus unicolor*** Sambar
C. axis unicolor Kerr, 1792: 300. TYPE-LOCALITY: Sri Lanka.

Local Names. *Sor pohu* (A), *Shiben* (Adi), *Sâchar* (Bangni/Nishi). *Tichi* (Bugun, all deer), *Dhu* (Idu Mishmi), *Gâsha* (Monpa), *Shawa* (Monpa, Zemithang area), *Zig* (Sherdukpen), *Chowk* (Wancho).

Distribution & Status. Common in the forests all over. Occurs in most of the protected areas. Population is, however, declining alarmingly outside the protected areas due to hunting.

Remarks. WPA: Schedule III.

138. *Cervus elaphus* Red deer, Shou
C. elphus Linnaeus, 1758: 67. TYPE-LOCALITY: Southern Sweden.

Distribution & Status. A stag was reported from the alpine pastures at above 4200 m elevation, north of Thingbu in Tawang dist in 1999 (C. Tsering, *pc*). Also reported from north of Magu, in the same district (Choudhury, 2002b). Past unconfirmed reports from the upper reaches of the Subansiri R. (Gee, 1964).

Subspecies. 138a. *C. e. wallichi* Shou, Sikkim stag, Tibetan red deer
C. wallichi Cuvier, 1823: 505. TYPE-LOCALITY: Nepal (or probably Mansarowar Lake, Nari-Khorsum dist, Tibet, according to Lydekker).

Remarks. The synonym, *C. affinis* Hodgson, 1841e: 721. (TYPE-LOCALITY: Saul Forest, Nepal), is often regarded as a separate subspecies. IUCN: DD.

(136) **139. *Axis porcinus*** Hog deer
Cervus porcinus Zimmermann, 1777: 532. TYPE-LOCALITY: Bengal.

Local Names. *Horina pohu, Hûgori pohu* (A), *Dûmsang* (Adi).

Distribution & Status. Common in the grasslands along the Siang, Dibang, Lohit, Deopani, Kamlang, Tengapani, Na-Dihing and Bor-Dikorai rivers. Stray animals are encountered elsewhere. Confined to the plains and adjacent foothills. The protected areas where the species occurs are Kamlang W.S., Pakhui W.S., D'Ering Memorial W.S., and Namdapha N.P. Other notable areas are Dibang, Lohit, Mebo, Pasighat, and Paya RFs.

Subspecies. 139a. *A. p. porcinus*. Nominate race.

Remarks. IUCN: LR (nt) (nominate race); WPA: Schedule III.

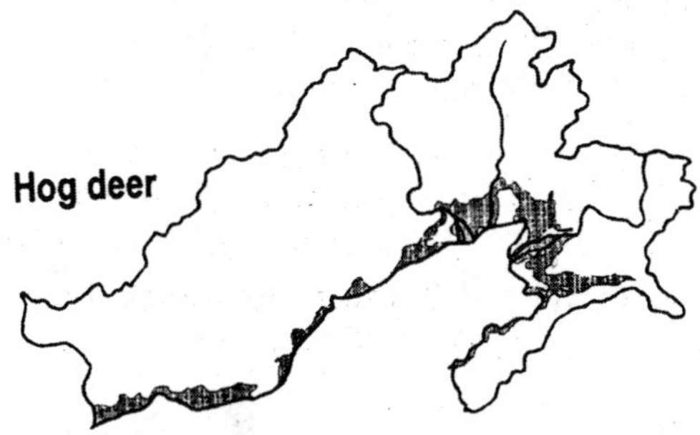

(137) **140. *Muntiacus muntjak*** Indian muntjak, Barking deer
Cervus muntjak Zimmermann, 1780: 131. TYPE-LOCALITY: Java, Indonesia. Conserved by Opinion 460 (1957).

Local Names. *Sâgoli pohu* (A), *Sîdum* (Adi), *Sadam* (Bangni/Nishi), *Kasha* (Monpa), *Skee* (Sherdukpen), *Meikhi* (Wancho).

Distribution & Status. Common all over, especially in the forests and scrub. Rare in the grasslands. It is the most abundant forest-dwelling deer in the area. Found in all the protected areas.

Subspecies. 140a. *M. m. vaginalis*
Cervus vaginalis Boddaert, 1785: 136. TYPE-LOCALITY: Bengal.

Remarks. WPA: Schedule III.

141. *Muntiacus crinifrons* Black muntjak
Cervulus crinifrons Sclater, 1885: 1, pl. 1. TYPE-LOCALITY: near Ningpo, Zhejiang, China.

Distribution & Status. In Gelling area of Upper Siang dist. Its occurrence in eastern and northern areas of Lohit dist is also certain.

Remarks. An addition to the mammals of India. Earlier known only from China (Lu & Sheng, 1984; Ohtaishi & Gao, 1990), however, recently discovered in N. Myanmar (Burma) from Hkakabo-Razi proposed N.P. (Rabinowitz *et al.*, 1998). This proposed national park is adjacent to and contiguous with Lohit dist. The form *gongshanensis* was recorded from Motuo and Medog in Tibet, which are almost right on the India-China border near Gelling.
CITES: Appendix I; IUCN: VU.

[***Muntiacus gongshanensis*** Gongshan muntjak
M. gongshanensis Ma, in Ma *et al.*, 1990: 47. TYPE-LOCALITY: Mijiao, Puladi, Gongshan County, N.W. Yunnan, 27°35′ N., 98°47′ E., China.

Remarks. Described as a new species (Ma *et al.*, 1990) but now considered a synonym of *M. crinifrons* (Amato *et al.*, 1999) although there is scope for further study. It has been recorded from many sites adjacent to Arunachal Pradesh including Bome County in E. Tibet (Wirth & Groves 1988). IUCN: DD.]

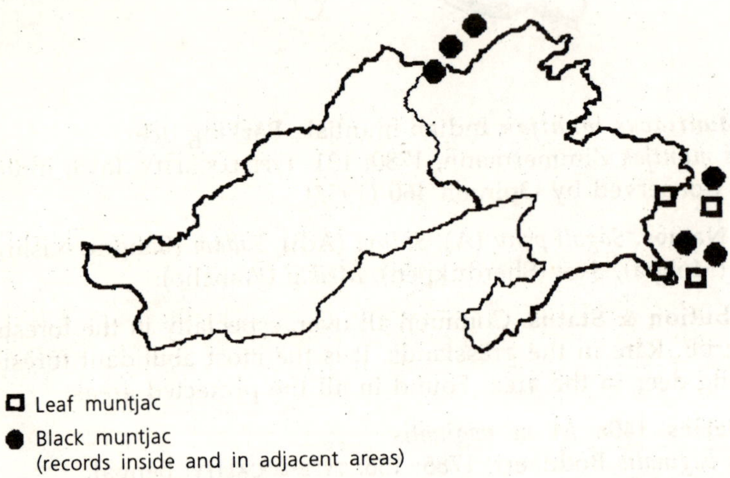

142. *Muntiacus putaoensis* Leaf muntjak
M. putaoensis. Amato *et al.*, 1999: 1–7. TYPE-LOCALITY: Hkakabo-Razi proposed N.P., N. Myanmar (Burma).

Distribution & Status. Known from only two records, one each in Lohit and Changlang (Vijaynagar area) districts. Likely to occur all along the eastern (border) areas of Lohit and Changlang districts. So far not recorded in any protected area although possible in Namdapha N.P. and Kamlang W.S.

Remarks. An addition to the mammals of India. This new species of deer has been discovered recently in N. Myanmar (Burma) from Hkakabo-Razi proposed N.P. (Rabinowitz *et al.*, 1998). This proposed national park is adjacent to and contiguous with Lohit dist having similar habitat on both sides of the international boundary.

Family BOVIDAE

Wild cattle, Sheep and Goats

Subfamily BOVINAE

(138) **143. *Bos gaurus*** Gaur, Indian 'bison'

B. gaurus Smith, H., 1827: 399. TYPE-LOCALITY: Mainpat, Surguja, Madhya Pradesh, India (originally recorded as Sarguja Tributary State) [23° N., 83° E.](Harper, 1940). Conserved by Opinion 1348 (1985).

Local Names. *Mithun, Methon* (A), *Bamui* (Adi, Mising), *Saling* (Bangni/Nishi), *Siya* (Bugun), *Borang mincha* (Monpa).

Distribution & Status. Fairly common in the forested hills and foothills all over, also in the grasslands. However, population declining all over due to habitat loss and poaching. Namdapha N.P. and Pakhui W.S. are the only protected areas having large populations (>300). Fairly large populations also occur in the reserved forests of Doimara, Papum, Dibang, Tengapani, Manabum and Kamlang. Other populations in protected areas are found in Eaglenest W.S., Sessa Orchid Sanctuary, D'Ering Memorial W.S. (in winter, mostly occasional), Mehao W.S. and Kamlang W.S.

Subspecies. 143a. *B. g. gaurus*. Nominate race.

Remarks. CITES: Appendix I; IUCN: VU; WPA: Schedule I . An interesting semi-domesticated derivative of *B. gaurus* occurs in N.E. India, Myanmar and S.E. Bangladesh. Popularly known as the Mithun or Gayal *Bos frontalis* Lambert, 1804: 57, it is well

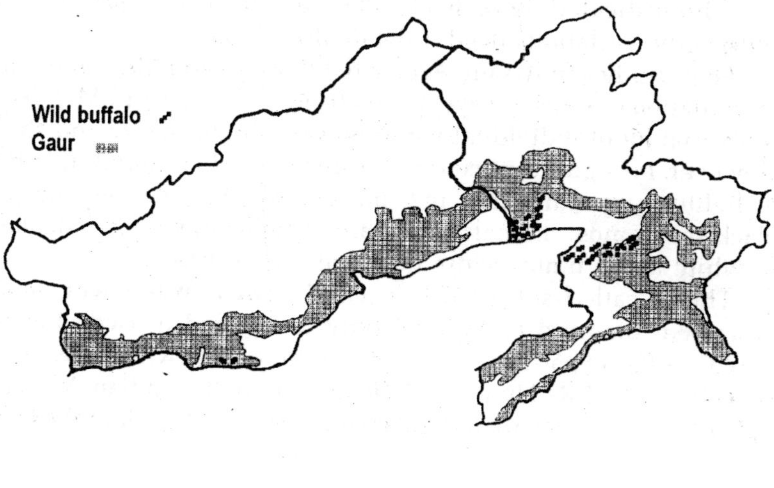

distributed all over Arunachal Pradesh in both domesticated as well as semi-wild form. It is generally believed that it is a cross between *B. gaurus* and domestic cattle. However, *B. frontalis* is infertile with *B. gaurus*. Corbet & Clutton-Brock (1984) treated it as a separate domestic species for the purpose of nomenclature rather than part of *B. gaurus* because it is clearly distinguishable from its wild cousin.

(139) **144. *Bubalus arnee*** Wild water buffalo, Asiatic wild buffalo
Bos arnee Kerr, 1792: 336. TYPE-LOCALITY: 'India, north from Bengal', restricted to Kuch Bihar (Harper, 1940). Apparently Koch Behar in northern West Bengal.

Local Names. *Bonoria moh* (A), *Gûnah* (A, lone bull), *Menjek* (Adi, Mising), *Mâji kâra* (Idu Mishmi).

Distribution & Status. Formerly widespread all over the grasslands along the Siang, Dibang, Lohit, Noa-Dihing, Kundil, Hajjo, Digaru, Sesseri, and Deopani rivers. Now confined mainly to a few pockets only, in the districts of E. Siang, Dibang Valley, Lohit and possibly E. Kameng. The main localities of occurrence are D'Ering Memorial W.S. (>100), Dibang R.F. (>100), Sirkee proposed R.F., Lai Anchal R.F., Kamlang R.F., ? Papum R.F., Mebo R.F., tract between D'Ering memorial W.S. and Sesseri R., and in the *chapories* of the Lohit R. from near Parshuramkund to Sunpura (Assam-Arunachal Pradesh border). Locally extinct in the valley of Noa-Dihing R.

Subspecies. 144a. *B. a. arnee*. Nominate race.

Remarks. So long described as *Bubalus bubalis* Linnaeus, 1758: 72, based upon a domestic specimen from Rome, Italy. The species was domesticated long back, may be prior to 2000 BC. The subspecific variations need a detailed review.

Field studies in Assam, Arunachal Pradesh and Meghalaya, and examination of museum specimens from N. Bengal and Meghalaya show that lot of individual variation exists in horn size and shape. However, no significant colour variation could be found. In a herd of lighter grey animals a few individuals may be very dark or blackish. In most animals, there are conspicuous white 'stocking' or white lower limbs below the knees and hocks.

The so-called subspecies, *B. bubalis fulvus* was never validly described. Blanford (1891) had only mentioned of two 'dun coloured' buffalo-heads from upper Assam, one of which was in the collection of M.R. Hume and the other in the Indian Museum, Calcutta. He also compared the characteristics of skull of these two specimens with the 'ordinary buffalo' (not wild buffalo !) and found some insignificant differences. CITES: Appendix II; IUCN: EN; WPA: Schedule I.

Subfamily CAPRINAE

145. *Budorcas taxicolor* Takin
B. taxicolor Hodgson, 1850: 65, pl. 1. TYPE-LOCALITY: Mishmi Hills, Arunachal Pradesh (originally recorded as N. Assam).

Local Names. *Siban, Takin* (Adi), *Akru* (Idu Mishmi), *Zewa* (Monpa), *Kemyak* (Monpa, Zemithang area; mistaken for wild yak).

Distribution & Status. Rare but found in many of the districts. Fairly common in the high elevation areas of Mishmi Hills in Dibang Valley and Lohit districts. Other districts where it has been recorded are Tawang, W. Kameng, E. Kameng, Upper Subansiri, Lower Subansiri, W. Siang, Upper Siang, and Lohit. Small population occurs in E. Siang, and Changlang districts. Protected areas where it has been recorded are Mouling N.P., Namdapha N.P., Dibang W.S., Kamlang W.S. and Mehao W.S.

Small number might have occasionally wandered in the higher areas of Eaglenest W.S. and Sessa Orchid Sanctuary. However, this movement has perhaps ceased due to habitat destruction and hunting. Usually occurs from 2500 to 4500 m but in winter may come down to 900 m also, especially in Dibang Valley dist.

Subspecies. 145a. *B. t. taxicolor*. The nominate race. Mishmi takin. The synonym, *B. t. whitei* Lydekker (1907b: 887. TYPE-LOCALITY: Bhutan) is also often regarded as a separate subspecies (Bhutan takin).

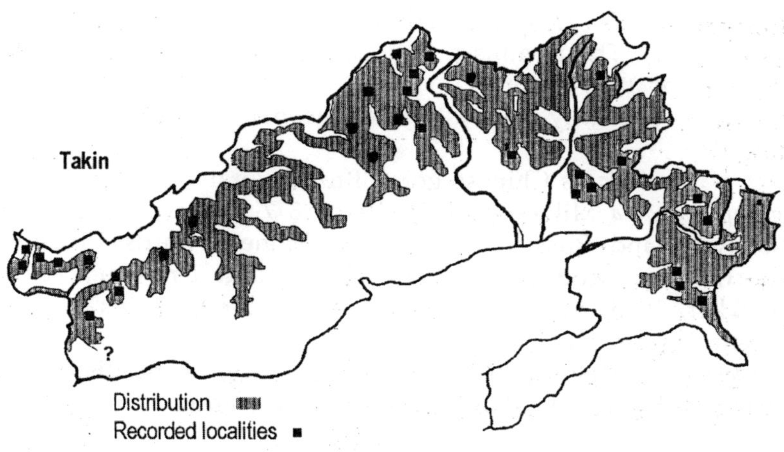

Remarks. CITES: Appendix II; IUCN: EN (ssp. *taxicolor*), VU (ssp. *whitei*); WPA: Schedule I.

(140) **146. *Naemorhedus goral*** Goral
Antilope goral Hardwicke, 1825a: 518. TYPE-LOCALITY: Nepal Himalaya.

Local Names. *Deo-sagoli* (A), *Siza* (Bugun), *Khing, Basha* (Monpa), *Zan* (Sherdukpen).

Distribution & Status. Common all over, usually above 900 m up. More common above 1500 m. Recorded up to 3000 m, occasionally above 4000 m. Found in all the the disricts. Protected areas where it has been recorded are Mouling N.P., Namdapha N.P., Dibang W.S., Eaglenest W.S., Kamlang W.S., Mehao W.S., Pakhui W.S., and Sessa Orchid Sanctuary. Also occurs near Tawang town.

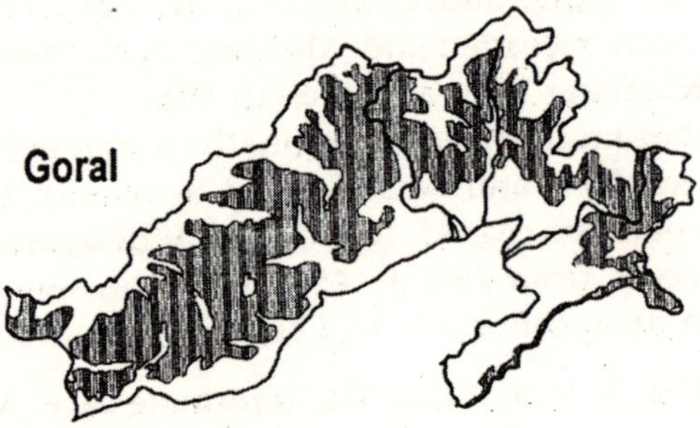

Subspecies. 146a. *N. g. goral* Himalayan goral, Grey goral
Antilope goral. The nominate race (syn: *N. hodgsoni* Pocock, 1908: 195. TYPE-LOCALITY: Sikkim).
All over, especially in western Arunachal Pradesh up to the Siang R.
146b. *N. g. caudatus* Chinese goral, Brown goral
Antilope caudata Milne-Edwards, 1867a: 377. TYPE-LOCALITY: Bureja Mts., Amurland, Russia (syn: *N. griseus* Milne-Edwards, 1872a: 93. TYPE-LOCALITY: Moupin, Sichuan, China; and *Urotragus evansi* Lydekker, 1905: 83. TYPE-LOCALITY: Mt. Victoria, Pokokku dist., Arakan, Myanmar).

Occurs in Mishmi Hills and Patkai Range, in the districts of Dibang Valley, Lohit, Changlang and Tirap (rare).

146c. *N. g. baileyi* Red goral
N. baileyi Pocock, 1914: 32. TYPE-LOCALITY: Dre, Yigrong Tso (Lake), Po Me, Tibet, 9000 ft. (syn: *N. cranbrooki* Hayman, 1961: 319. TYPE-LOCALITY: Adung Valley, N. Myanmar (Burma), 28°10′ N., 97°40′ E., 8000 ft).

Occurs in Mishmi Hills, in the districts of Dibang Valley and Lohit.

Remarks. Groves & Grubb (1985) threated these three as separate species. CITES: Appendix I; IUCN: LR (ssp. *goral*), VU (as sp. *caudatus*), VU (as sp. *baileyi*); WPA: Schedule I.

(141) **147. *Capricornis sumatraensis*** Serow
Antilope sumatraensis Bechstein, 1799: 98. TYPE-LOCALITY: Sumatra, Indonesia.

Local Names. *Deo-sagoli, Bonoria sagoli* (A), *Bibe* (Adi), *Gophu* (Aka), *Shrai* (Bugun), *Manjo* (Idu Mishmi), *Shubroi* (Miji), *Kyah* (Monpa), *Shara* (Sherdukpen), *Meiza* (Wancho).

Distribution & Status. Common all over Arunachal Pradesh, occurring in all the districts, between 300 and 3100 m, occasionally down to 100 m also. Protected areas where it has been recorded are Mouling N.P., Namdapha N.P., Dibang W.S., Eaglenest W.S., Itanagar W.S., Kamlang W.S., Mehao W.S., Pakhui W.S., Sessa Orchid Sanctuary and Taley Valley W.S.

Subspecies. 147a. *C. s. jamrachi* Pocock, 1908: 183. Himalayan serow. TYPE-LOCALITY: Kalimpong, Darjeeling dist, West Bengal, India (syn: *Antilope thar* Hodgson, 1831: 324. TYPE-LOCALITY: Nepal Himalaya).

This subspecies is characterised by dark-grey body colour. Occurs in the Himalayas and Mishmi Hills, in the districts of Tawang, W. Kameng, E. Kameng, Upper Subansiri, Lower Subansiri, Papum Pare, Upper Siang, E. Siang, W. Siang, Dibang Valley and northern areas of Lohit.

Heads and horns of some Caprini recorded, or are likely to occur in Arunachal Pradesh, illustrating different horn types. Takin (top left), bharal (top right), nayan (centre), goral (bottom left), serow (bottom right).

147b. *C. s. rubidus*
C. rubida Blyth, 1863: 174. Burmese serow, Red serow. TYPE-LOCALITY: Arakan Hills, Burma (Myanmar).
Body colour is reddish-brown. Occurs in the Patkai Range and also perhaps Dapha Bum, in the districts of Tirap, Changlang and also perhaps the southern areas of Lohit.

Remarks. Included in the genus *Capricornis* (Ogilby, 1837; Blyth, 1863; Ellerman & Morrison-Scott, 1951). However, Groves & Grubb (1985) suggest its inclusion in the genus *Naemorhedus*. The colour difference between the two races found in N.E. India is conspicuous. *C. s. jamrachi* of the north bank (of the Brahmaputra

and Lohit rivers) is dark-grey while *rubidus* of the south bank is chestnut-brown or reddish-brown.
CITES: Appendix I; IUCN: VU (ssp. *jamrachi/thar:* VU; *rubidus*: EN); WPA: Schedule I.

148. *Pseùdois nayaur* Bharal, Blue sheep
Ovis nayaur Hodgson, 1833b: 135. TYPE-LOCALITY: Tibetan frontier of Nepal.

Local Name. *Nâwa* (Monpa).

Distribution & Status. Rare and restricted to the higher areas of the Great Himalaya and Mishmi Hills. Specific records from Tawang (Singh, 1991), W. Kameng and E. Kameng districts (AUC). Occurrence near the India-China border in Dibang Valley and Lohit districts is almost certain due to records from adjacent areas of China and N. Myanmar (Burma) (Rabinowitz & Khaing, 1998). No doubt, occurs in small numbers in Upper Subansiri, Lower Subansiri and Upper Siang districts also. Usually occurs above 3500 m to up to 5500 m, affecting alpine meadows above timberline. In winter, may come down to a little lower. So far not recorded in any of the protected areas, however, likely to occur in the highest parts of Namdapha N.P., Dibang W.S., and Kamlang W.S. Also perhaps in Dichu R.F.

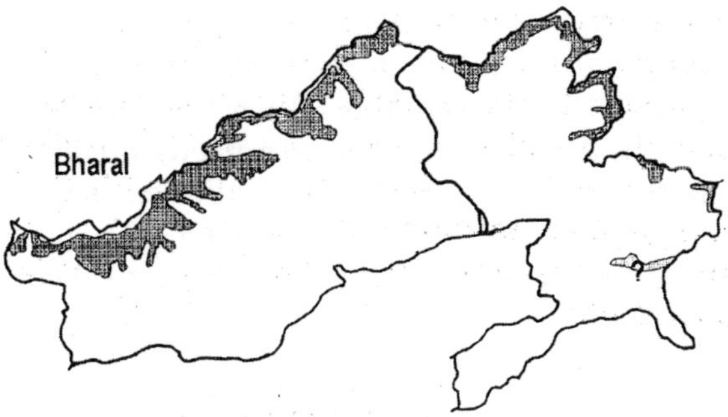

Subspecies. 148a *P. n. nayaur.* The nominate subspecies.

Remarks. IUCN: LR (nt); WPA: Schedule I.

[***Ovis ammon*** Nayan, Argali
Capra ammon Linnaeus, 1758: 70. TYPE-LOCALITY: Altai Mountains, near Ust-Kamenogorsk, on the Irtish Rver, Semipalatinsk, Kazakhstan.

Local Names. ? *Nâwa* (Monpa).

Distribution & Status. So far no specimen record. Reported from the Great and trans-Himalaya in western Arunachal Pradesh, especially along the India-China border in Tawang, W. Kameng and E. Kameng districts (AUC). Not found in any of the protected areas.

Subspecies. *O. a. hodgsonii* Nayan, Great Tibetan sheep, Tibetan argali.
O. hodgsonii Blyth, 1841: 65. TYPE-LOCALITY: Tibet, probably on Nepal frontier (Lydekker).

Remarks. Local hunters confuse Nayan with that of Bharal. CITES: Appendix I; IUCN: VU (ssp. *hodgsonii*); WPA: Schedule I.]

Order RODENTIA

Rodents

The order Rodentia, rodents or gnawing animals include the squirrels, rats and mice, porcupines, and their allies. This is also the largest order of mammals both worldwide and in Arunachal Pradesh. These small mammals are distinguished from all other mammals by their distinctive teeth, i.e., a single pair of incisors above and below that are chisel-edged and ever-growing, separated by a long diastema (canines absent) from a compact row of three to five (rarely one or two) cheek-teeth. Recent reviews of different aspects of this order include contributors to the volume edited by Luckett & Hartenberger (1985) and Jaeger (1988). The classification of rodents is unstable and needs further review. The order is represented by as many as 53 different species or about 25% of the mammals included in this checklist. The rodents can easily adapt to almost any type of surrounding except for the extreme polar regions.

Family SCIURIDAE

Squirrels

Subfamily RATUFINAE

Giant squirrels

(142) **149. *Ratufa bicolor*** Malayan giant squirrel, Black giant squirrel
Sciurus bicolor Sparrman, 1778: 70. TYPE-LOCALITY: Anjer, W. Java, Indonesia.

R. bicolor

Local Names. *Chikkat, Lippo* (Adi), *Papiang* (Bugun), *Subge* (Miji).

Distribution & Status. Found in the forests all over Arunachal Pradesh, from plains to mountains (from 100 to up to 2400 m). Common in well forested areas. Found in most of the protected areas.

Subspecies. 149a. *R. b. gigantea*
Sciurus giganteus M'Clelland, 1839: 150. TYPE-LOCALITY: Assam.

Remarks. CITES: Appendix II; WPA: Schedule II (II).

Subfamily CALLOSCIURINAE

(143) **150. *Callosciurus erythraeus*** Pallas's squirrel
Sciurus erythraeus Pallas, 1779: 377. TYPE-LOCALITY: Garo Hills, Meghalaya (originally recorded as Assam) (restricted by Moore & Tate, 1965).

Local Names. *Kerketua* (A, all squirrels), *Thrui* (Bugun).

Distribution & Status. Common all over, in the forested plains, hills and mountains, up to above 3000 m.

Subspecies. At least four are likely to occur in the area.
150a. *C. e. intermedius* Red-bellied squirrel
Sciurus gordoni var. *intermedia* Anderson, 1879: 241. TYPE-LOCALITY: Dikrang Valley (Lakhimpur dist), Assam.
150b. *C. e. bhutanensis*
Sciurus erythraeus bhutanensis Bonhote, 1901: 161. TYPE-LOCALITY: Bhutan.

150c. *C.e. nagarum* Thomas & Wroughton, 1916: 228. TYPE-LOCALITY: Sadiya, Tinsukia dist, Assam.
150d. *C.e. aquilo*
C. castaneoventris aquilo Wroughton, 1921a: 601. Dibang R., Dibang Valley dist, Arunachal Pradesh, 600 ft. (originally recorded as Sadiya [mispelt as Adiya in Corbet & Hill, 1992], Assam).

Remarks. Subspecific variations need a detailed review. Although detailed descriptions were given by Moore & Tate (1965), the complex geographical variation is still confusing unless mapped on a larger scale. The characteristics common to all subspecies is·contrasting venter (reddish, maroon to creamy buff). *C. gordoni* which has been listed as a species by Ghosh (1987) is conspecific with *C. erythraeus*.

(144) **151. *Callosciurus pygerythrus*** Irrawaddy squirrel, Himalayan hoary-bellied squirrel
Sciurus pygerythrus Geoffroy, 1831: 145, pl. 7. TYPE-LOCALITY: Pegu, Burma (Myanmar).

Distribution & Status. Common all over in the forested hills and plains, usually occurs below 1700 m. Also affects village and semi-urban woodlands. The probable range of different subspecies are, *lokroides* in western Arunachal Pradesh, *blythi* in extreme eastern areas while *stevensi* in the rest of the state.

Subspecies. At least three are likely to occur in the area.
151a. *C. p. lokroides*
Sciurus lokroides Hodgson, 1836: 232. TYPE-LOCALITY: Nepal.
151b. *C. p. blythi*
Sciurus blythii Tytler, 1854: 172. TYPE-LOCALITY: Dhaka, Bangladesh.
151c. *C. p. stevensi*
Sciurus stevensi Thomas, 1908: 246. TYPE-LOCALITY: Beni-Chang, Abor-Miri Hills, Arunachal Pradesh (originally recorded as N. Assam), 4000 ft.

Remarks. The species is sympatric with *P. erythraeus* except in the village woodlands where latter is not found. Subspecific variations not prominent and further review is necessary. IUCN: VU.

(145) **152. *Tamiops mcclellandii*** Himalayan striped squirrel
Sciurus mcclellandii Horsfield, 1840: 152. TYPE-LOCALITY: Assam.

Distribution & Status. Common in the forested hills and plains. Recorded up to 2500 m. May also occur higher.

Subspecies. At least three are recognised (Moore & Tate, 1965) of which only one occurs in the area.
153a. *T. m. mcclellandii.* Nominate race.

(146) **153. *Dremomys lokriah*** Orange-bellied Himalayan squirrel
Sciurus lokriah Hodgson, 1836: 232. TYPE-LOCALITY: Nepal.

Distribution & Status. Found in the forested hills and foothills, up to 2700 m. Not uncommon at suitable localities.

Subspecies. At least three occur in the area.
153a. *D. l. lokriah.* Nominate race.
153b. *D. l. macmillani*
D. macmillani Thomas & Wroughton, 1916: 238. TYPE-LOCALITY: Tatkon, W. Burma (Myanmar).
153c. *D. l. subflaviventris* Thomas, 1922b: 429. TYPE-LOCALITY: Assam.

Remarks. The subspecific classification needs a detailed review. Moore & Tate (1965) recognized four subspecies including *D. l. garonum* and *D. l. macmillani* while Corbet & Hill (1992) proposes six (including the nominate race) which excludes *D. l. macmillani.* In the N. bank of the Brahmaputra R., it is mostly the nominate subspecies while in the south bank, i.e., in eastern Arunachal Pradesh, the other two subspecies are found.

(147) **154. *Dremomys pernyi*** Perny's long-nosed squirrel
Sciurus pernyi Milne-Edwards, 1867b: 230, pl. 19. TYPE-LOCALITY: Sichuan, China

Distribution & Status. Found mainly in the foothills and mountains up to 3500 m up. Exact status unclear, may be rare.

Subspecies. 154a. *D. p. howelli* Thomas, 1922a: 401. TYPE-LOCALITY: Machangkai, 25 miles S.W. of Tengyueh, S.W. Yunnan, China.

Remarks. Corbet & Hill (1992) suggest that the subspecies *howelli* is likely to occur in Arunachal Pradesh and not the nominate race which has been mentioned in Ellerman & Morrison-Scott (1951).

(148) **155. *Dremomys rufigenis*** Red-cheeked squirrel
Sciurus rufigenis Blanford, 1878: 156, pl. VIII. TYPE-LOCALITY: Mt. Mulaiyit, Tenasserim, S. Burma (Myanmar).

Distribution & Status. Mainly a montane species. Exact status in Arunachal Pradesh is unclear but occurs, especially in the eastern areas. Recorded from Namdapha N.P. (Ghosh, 1987).

Subfamily MARMOTINAE

156. *Marmota bobak* Himalayan marmot
Mus bobak Müller, 1776: 40. TYPE-LOCALITY: Poland.

Local Name. *Shippa* (Monpa).

Distribution & Status. Specifically recorded from Thingbu area (Singh, 1991) and higher elevations in Zemithang area of Tawang district, and in the northern areas of W. Kameng dist. Very likely to occur all along the India-China border, between 4000 and 5500 m.

Subspecies. 156a *M. b. himalayana.*
Arctomys himalayanus Hodgson, 1841e: 777. TYPE-LOCALITY: Nepal.

Himalayan marmot

Probable distribution ▦
Recorded localities ■

Family PTEROMYIDAE

Flying squirrels

(149) **157. *Trogopterus pearsonii*** Hairy-footed flying squirrel
Sciuropterus pearsonii Gray, 1842: 263. TYPE-LOCALITY: Darjeeling, West Bengal, India.

Local Names. (Generally for all flying squirrels). *Bângkek* (A), *Sibyong* (Adi), *Dichai, Thring* (Bugun), *Chuowa-changkor* (Monpa), *Songo* (Monpa, Zemithang area), *Khiaw* (Sherdukpen).

Distribution & Status. Widely distributed in the forests in the hills, between 900 and 2400 m elevation.

Remarks. Earlier it was included in the genus *Belomys* which is now considered synonymous with the genus *Trogopterus*. IUCN: LR (nt). WPA: Schedule II (II).

(150) **158. *Petaurista petaurista*** Common giant flying squirrel, Red flying squirrel
Sciurus petaurista Pallas, 1766: 54. TYPE-LOCALITY: W. Java, Indonesia.

Local Name. *Hojo* (Adi).

Distribution & Status. Common in the forested plains and hills, from 100 to above 1500 m. Very common in the primary forests in the foothills.

Subspecies. 158a. *P. p. albiventer*
Pteromys albiventer Gray, 1834 (in 1830–35): pl. 18. TYPE-LOCALITY: Nepal.

Remarks. No detailed review is available on subspecific variation. *P. alborufus* was also believed to occur in Assam including eastern Arunachal Pradesh (the race *candidulas*) (Choudhury, 1994a) as Ellerman & Morrison-Scott (1951) considered *candidulus* to be a subspecies of *alborufus*. Subsequently on the basis of external and dental characters, they are included in *P. petaurista* (Corbet & Hill, 1992). WPA: Schedule II (II).

(151) **159. *Petaurista philippensis***
Pteromys philippensis Elliot, 1839: 217. TYPE-LOCALITY: near Madras, Tamil Nadu, India.

Distribution & Status. Imperfectly known. Likely to occur all over.

Remarks. Very similar to *P. petaurista* and field identification rather difficult. Subspecific classification needs a review. WPA: Schedule II (II).

160. *Petaurista elegans* Lesser giant flying squirrel
Pteromys elegans Temminck, 1836: XII. TYPE-LOCALITY: Nusa Kumbangan I, S. Java.

Distribution & Status. Recorded from Namdapha N.P. (Ghosh, 1987).

Remarks. WPA: Schedule II (II).

(152) **161. *Petaurista caniceps*** Grey-headed giant flying squirrel, Lesser giant flying squirrel
Sciuropterus caniceps Gray, 1842: 262. TYPE-LOCALITY: Nepal.

Distribution & Status. A montane species, occurs up to 3600 m in the Himalaya and Mishmi Hills.

Remarks. Ellerman & Morrison-Scott (1951) included it in *P. elegans*. WPA: Schedule II (II).

162. *Petaurista magnificus* Hodgson's flying squirrel
Sciuropterus magnificus Hodgson, 1836: 231. TYPE-LOCALITY: Nepal.

Distribution & Status. Reported from Mouling N.P. (Chatterjee, 1989) and also elsewhere from Siang area (Katti *et al.*, 1990). There are specimen records from E. Bhutan, between 1525 and 2500 m (Chakraborty, 1975) which are not far from the western boundary of Arunachal Pradesh.

Remarks. Corbet & Hill (1992) mentioned of its occurrence from Nepal to Darjeeling only. WPA: Schedule II (II). IUCN: LR (nt).

163. *Petaurista nobilis*
Sciuropterus nobilis Gray, 1842: 263. TYPE-LOCALITY: Darjeeling, West Bengal, India.

Distribution & Status. A montane species, occurring in the higher hills and mountains. Recorded in W. Kameng district including higher areas of Eaglenest W.S. and Sessa Orchid Sanctuary occurring between 1500–2300 m in subtropical and temperate broadleaf forest (Choudhury 2002a). Also recorded in Tawang district (AUC). In C. Nepal and Bhutan, recorded at *c.* 1670–300 m.

Subspecies. At least two are recognised (Ghose & Saha, 1981) of which only one occurs in the area.
163a. *P. n. singhei* Saha, 1977: 27. TYPE-LOCALITY: Gomchu, Gomchu Valley, Bhutan (*c.* 2286 m).

Remarks. An addition to the mammals of N.E. India. Earlier known only from C. Nepal to Bhutan. Differs from the nominate race in having larger size, richer colour and lack of pale mid-dorsal stripe. Some include it in *P. magnificus*. WPA: Schedule II (II). IUCN: LR (nt).

164. *Eupetaurus cinereus* Woolly flying squirrel
E. cinereus Thomas, 1888: 258. TYPE-LOCALITY: Gilgit Valley, Kashmir.

Distribution & Status. A montane species. No specimen record so far but its presence is indicated by its distribution pattern ranging from Pakistan to S. China all along the Himalaya. In N. Sikkim, recorded at 3000 m (Agrawal & Chakraborty, 1970).

Remarks. WPA: Schedule II (II).

165. *Biswamoyopterus biswasi* Namdapha flying squirrel
B. biswasi Saha, 1981: 333. TYPE-LOCALITY: Deban, 26 km E. of Miao, Namdapha N.P., Arunachal Pradesh (350 m).

Distribution & Status. Known only from the type locality in Namdapha N.P., Changlang dist. Till now endemic to Arunachal Pradesh.

Remarks. Its entire white underside (with faint orange-rufous tint on the patagium) distinguishes it from the other sympatric large flying squirrels. Known only from the holotype. IUCN: CR.

(153) **166. *Hylopetes alboniger*** Particoloured flying squirrel
Sciuropterus alboniger Hodgson, 1836: 231. TYPE-LOCALITY: Nepal.

Distribution & Status. In the forests and adjacent countryside, from plains to hills, up to about 3000 m. In Tinsukia dist, eastern Assam, recorded at 120 m elevation on flat plains (Choudhury, 1995b).

Subspecies. 166a. *H. a. alboniger*. Nominate race.

Remarks. IUCN: EN; WPA: Schedule II (II).

Family MURIDAE

Rats and Mice

Subfamily MURINAE

Rats and Mice

(154) **167. *Mus musculus*** House mouse
M. musculus Linnaeus, 1758: 62. TYPE-LOCALITY: Upsala, Sweden.

Local Names. *Nîgoni* (A, all mice and rats).

Distribution & Status. Very common all over, from plains to mountains. Recorded up to 4200 m elevation.

Subspecies. At least three occur in the area.
167a. *M. m. castaneus*
M. castaneus Waterhouse, 1843: 134. TYPE-LOCALITY: Philippines.
167b. *M. m. homourus*
M. homourus Hodgson, 1845: 268. (Outdoor type). TYPE-LOCALITY: Nepal.

167c. *M. m. urbanus*
M. urbanus Hodgson, 1845: 269. (Indoor type). TYPE-LOCALITY: Kathmandu, Nepal.

Remarks. WPA: Schedule V (all rats and mice).

168. *Mus booduga* Little Indian field mouse
Leggada booduga Gray, 1837: 586. TYPE-LOCALITY: S. Mahratta country, India.

Distribution & Status. Found all over, may be above 3000 m also as in the Kumaon and Garhwal (U.P.) Himalaya, recorded up to 3695 m (Mandal, 1984).

(155) **169. *Mus cookii***
M. cookii Ryley, 1914: 664. TYPE-LOCALITY: Gokteik, Shan States, Burma (Myanmar), 2133 ft.

Distribution & Status. Mainly a montane species. Found but exact status unclear. Specimen records from Namdapha N.P. (Ghosh, 1987).

Subspecies. 169a. *M. c. nagarum*
Leggada nagarum Thomas, 1921a: 597. TYPE-LOCALITY: recorded as Golaghat, Naga Hills, Assam, 300 ft (the location may be near Assam-Nagaland border or in Karbi Anglong, Assam).

Remarks. *M. cookii* was considered earlier as a race of *M. famulus* while *M. cookii nagarum* was included as a subspecies of *M. cervicolor* (Ellerman & Morrison-Scott, 1951).

(156) **170. *Mus cervicolor*** Fawn-coloured mouse
M. cervicolor Hodgson, 1845: 268. TYPE-LOCALITY: Nepal.

Distribution & Status. Occurs in the hills and mountains. Recorded between 1150 and 3200 m elevation (Abe, 1977).

(158) **171. *Mus pahari*** Sikkim mouse
M. pahari Thomas, 1916a: 415. TYPE-LOCALITY: Batasia, Sikkim, India, 6000 ft.

Distribution & Status. Found all over, from edge of the plains to mountains. Not uncommon.

Subspecies. Usually three are recognised, of which two occur in the area.

171a. *M. p. pahari.* Nominate race.
171b. *M. p. jacksoniae*
Leggada jacksoniae Thomas, 1921a: 596. TYPE-LOCALITY: Laitkynsao, Khasi Hills, Meghalaya (originally recorded as Assam), India.

(159) **172. *Vandeleuria oleracea*** Palm mouse, Indian long-tailed tree mouse
Mus oleraceus Bennett, 1832: 121. TYPE-LOCALITY: Deccan, India.

Distribution & Status. Found all over, mainly in the forests. Not uncommon from plains to up to *c.* 2500 m.

Subspecies. 172a. *V. o. dumeticola*
Mus dumeticola Hodgson, 1845: 268. TYPE-LOCALITY: Nepal.

(160) **173. *Rattus rattus*** House rat, Black rat, Roof rat, Ship rat
Mus rattus Linnaeus, 1758: 61. TYPE-LOCALITY: Sweden.

Local Names. (Generally for all rats). *Endur* (A), *Thung* (Bugun), *Chuh* (Monpa), *Judha* (Monpa, Zemithang area).

Distribution & Status. Very common all over.

Subspecies. 173a. *R. r. brunneusculus*
Mus brunneusculus Hodgson, 1845: 267. TYPE-LOCALITY: Nepal.
173b. *R. r. tistae* Hinton, 1918: 68. TYPE-LOCALITY: Pashok, Sikkim, India.
173c. *R. r. bhotia* Hinton, 1918: 72. TYPE-LOCALITY: Hasimara, Jalpaiguri dist., West Bengal, India (originally recorded as Bhutan *Duars*).

Remarks. The subspecific status in the area needs a detailed review. A serious pest of crops and stored food.

(161) **174. *Rattus nitidus*** Himalayan rat
Mus nitidus Hodgson, 1845: 267. TYPE-LOCALITY: Nepal.

Distribution & Status. Widely distributed, up to above 2500 m. There is an exceptional record at 3900 m in Yunnan, China (Wang *et al.*, 1985). Also found in village houses.

Remarks. May be confused with *R. rattus* and *R. turkestanicus.* Presence of six pairs of teats, including two well-separated post-axillary ones on each side distinduighes it from *R. rattus;* and from *R. turkestanicus* by soft, spineless pelage and almost white hind feet.

(162) **175. *Rattus remotus***
Epimys remotus Robinson & Kloss, 1914: 231. TYPE-LOCALITY: Samui I, E. peninsular Thailand.

Distribution & Status. Mainly a rat of the forests. Widespread all over.

Remarks. Also described and mapped as *R. sikkimensis* (Hinton, 1919; Musser & Heaney, 1985). Differs from similar looking *R. rattus* by longer black hair in the mid-dorsal line, white ventrum, etc.

(163) **176. *Rattus turkestanicus***
Mus rattoides Hodgson, 1845: 267. TYPE-LOCALITY: Nepal. Preoccupied by *Mus rattoides* Pictet & Pictet, 1844, a form of *Rattus rattus* in Brazil (Schlitter & Thonglongya, 1971).

Distribution & Status. A high-elevation species affecting vicinity of human habitation in the hills and mountains across Arunachal Pradesh. Occurs up to *c.* 4200 m elevation.

(164) **177. *Golunda ellioti*** Indian bush rat
G. ellioti Gray, 1837: 586. TYPE-LOCALITY: Dharwar, India.

Distribution & Status. So far no specific record, however, likely to occur in the foothills and edge of the plains in W. Arunachal Pradesh. Mainly found in grass and scrub including abandoned *jhum* fields.

(165) **178. *Bandicota indica*** Large bandicoot-rat
Mus indicus Bechstein, 1800: 497. TYPE-LOCALITY: Pondicherry, India.

Distribution & Status. Found all over, especially in the plains and foothills. Not uncommon.

Subspecies. 178a. *B. i. nemorivagus*
Mus (Rattus) nemorivagus Hodgson, 1836: 234. TYPE-LOCALITY: Nepal.

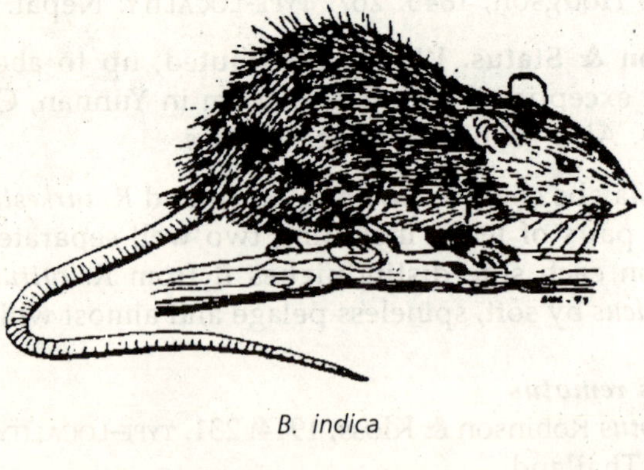

B. indica

(166) **179. *Bandicota bengalensis*** Lesser bandicoot-rat, "Indian mole rat"
Arvicola bengalensis Gray, 1835 (in 1830–35): pl. 21. TYPE-LOCALITY: Bengal, India.

Distribution & Status. Common and widespread in the plains and at the base of the hills. A serious pest to crops as well as stored food.

(167) **180. *Chiropodomys gliroides*** Pencil-tailed tree mouse
Mus gliroides Blyth, 1856: 721. TYPE-LOCALITY: Cherrapunji, Khasi Hills, Meghalaya.

Distribution & Status. Mainly found in the foothills and lower hills.

(168) **181. *Micromys minutus*** Harvest mouse
Mus minutus Pallas, 1771: 454. TYPE-LOCALITY: Simbirsk, R. Volga, Russia.

Distribution & Status. Common all over, from plains to up to *c.* 2000 m.

Subspecies. 181a. *M. m. erythrotis*
Mus erythrotis Blyth, 1856: 721. TYPE-LOCALITY: Cherrapunji, Khasi Hills, Meghalaya.

Remarks. IUCN: LR (nt).

[***Apodemus sylvaticus*** Wood mouse, Common field mouse
Mus sylvaticus Linnaeus, 1758: 62. TYPE-LOCALITY: Upsala, Sweden.

Remarks. Ellerman & Morrison-Scott (1951) included Assam (Mishmi Hills in Arunachal Pradesh) within its range (form *orestes* assigning it subspecific status) but Corbet & Hill (1992) treated *orestes* as a full species while Musser & Carleton (1993) included it in *A. draco* as a synonym. Hence, it is unlikely that *A. sylvaticus* occurs within the limits of N.E. India. The nearest site is C. Nepal].

(169) **182. *Apodemus draco***
Mus sylvaticus draco Barrett-Hamilton, 1900: 417. TYPE-LOCALITY: Kuatun, Fujian, S.E. China.

Distribution & Status. Mainly found in E. Arunachal Pradesh, i.e., in Mishmi Hills.

(170) **183. *Apodemus orestes***
A. speciosus orestes Thomas, 1911c: 49 (and 1912: 136). TYPE-LOCALITY: Mt. Omei Shan, Sichuan, China.

Distribution & Status. Known from Mishmi Hills of eastern Arunachal Pradesh (recorded as Assam in most of the publications). Usually occurs in the hills and mountains. Recorded up to 3400 m in Yunnan (Corbet & Hill, 1992).

Remarks. Earlier included as a subspecies of *A. sylvaticus* (Ellerman & Morrison-Scott, 1951).

184. *Apodemus latronum*
A. speciosus latronum Thomas, 1911c: 49 (and 1912b: 137). TYPE-LOCALITY: Tatsienlu, W. Sichuan, China.

Distribution & Status. Mainly a high elevation species. Occurs between 2700 and 4000 m in Yunnan (Corbet & Hill, 1992). In Arunachal Pradesh, found in eastern areas, especially in Mishmi Hills.

(172) **185. *Dacnomys millardi*** Millard's rat, Large-toothed rat
D. millardi Thomas, 1916a: 405. TYPE-LOCALITY: Gopaldhara, near Darjeeling, West Bengal, 3440 ft.

Local Names. *Kobu* (Adi, all rats).

Distribution & Status. Mostly in the hills, all over. There are specimen records from Mishmi Hills (Thomas, 1922b) and Namdapha N.P. (Ghosh, 1987).

Subspecies. 185a. *D. m. millardi*. Nominate race.
185b. *D. m. wroughtoni*
D. wroughtoni Thomas, 1922b: 430. TYPE-LOCALITY: Dreyi, Mishmi Hills, Arunachal Pradesh, 6000 ft (originally recorded as N. Assam).

(174) **186. *Niviventer niviventer*** White-bellied rat
Mus (Rattus) niviventer Hodgson, 1836: 234. TYPE-LOCALITY: Kathmandu, Nepal.

Distribution & Status. Found all over Arunachal Pradesh, from foothills to above 3000 m. Among the commoner of the rats. Often trapped with snares for food.

Remarks. This genus was earlier included in *Rattus* (Ellerman & Morrison-Scott, 1951). Corbet & Hill (1992) mentioned of its range from Pakistan to Nepal.

(175) **187. *Niviventer tenaster***
Epimys tenaster Thomas, 1916b: 425. TYPE-LOCALITY: Mt. Muleyit, Tenasserim, Burma (Myanmar), 5000–6000 ft.

Distribution & Status. Status unclear but found.

Remarks. Earlier included as a subspecies of *Rattus cremoriventer* (Ellerman & Morrison-Scott, 1951).

(176) **188. *Niviventer fulvescens*** Chestnut rat
Mus fulvescens Gray, 1847a: 18. TYPE-LOCALITY: Nepal.

Distribution & Status. Mostly found in the hills and foothills, from 1000 to 2500 m elevations.

Remarks. *Rattus jerdoni*, as listed in Ghosh (1987) is conspecific with *N. fulvescens.*

(177) **189. *Niviventer brahma***
Epimys brahma Thomas, 1914b: 232. TYPE-LOCALITY: Anzong Valley, Mishmi Hills, Arunachal Pradesh (originally recorded as Assam), India, 6000 ft.

Distribution & Status. Found in Mishmi Hills, in the districts of Dibang Valley, part of E. Siang and Lohit. Status in other parts unknown.

Remarks. Ellerman & Morrison-Scott (1951) included it as a subspecies of *Rattus fulvescens*. Closely related to *N. eha*.

190. *Niviventer eha* Smoke-bellied rat
Epimys eha Wroughton, 1916c: 428. TYPE-LOCALITY: Lachen, Sikkim, 8800 ft.

Distribution & Status. Mostly in the mountains, preferring damp forest from 2600 m up. In Nepal, recorded at 2600–3700 m (Corbet & Hill, 1992).

(178) **191. *Niviventer langbianis***
Rattus cremoriventer langbianis Robinson & Kloss, 1922: 90. TYPE-LOCALITY: Langbian Peaks, Annam, Vietnam.

Distribution & Status. Status unclear but found, especially in E. Arunachal Pradesh.

Remarks. Marshall (1976) and Dao & Cao (1990) treated it as a race of *R. cremoriventer* but Musser (1981) recognised it as a separate species.

192 *Niviventer andersoni*
Epimys andersoni Thomas, 1911a: 4 (and 1911b: 171). TYPE-LOCALITY: Omei-San, Sichuan, China.

Distribution & Status. Status unclear but likely to occur as has been recor-ded from E. Tibet, close to India-China border. A high elevation species.

(179) **193. *Leopoldamys edwardsi*** Noisy rat, Long-tailed giant rat
Mus edwardsi Thomas, 1882: 587. TYPE-LOCALITY: Mountains of W. Fujian (probably Kuatun), China.

Distribution & Status. Well distributed in the hills and foothills.

Subspecies. 193a. *L. e. garonum*
Rattus listeri garonum Thomas, 1921b: 27. TYPE-LOCALITY: Tura, Garo Hills, Meghalaya (earlier recorded as Assam), India, 1400 ft.

Remarks. *L.e. garonum* was considered as a subspecies of *L. sabanus* (Ellerman & Morrision-Scott, 1951).

(180) **194. *Berylmys manipulus*** Manipur rat
Epimys manipulus Thomas, 1916a: 413. TYPE-LOCALITY: Kampat, Kabaw Valley, 20 miles W. of Kindat, W. Burma (Myanmar), 600 ft.

Distribution & Status. Hills and foothills south of the Brahmaputra R., especially in E. Arunachal Pradesh (Patkai Range, etc). Specimen record from Namdapha N.P. (Ghosh, 1987).

Remarks. Considered as a separate genus by Musser & Newcomb (1983). Earlier included in *Rattus* (Ellerman & Morrison-Scott, 1951).

(181) **195. *Berylmys mackenziei***
Epimys mackenziei Thomas 1916a: 410. TYPE-LOCALITY: Haingyan, 50 Miles W. of Kindat, Chin Hills, Burma (Myanmar).

Distribution & Status. Found but exact status unclear. Perhaps mainly in the S. bank of the Brahmaputra R., especially in E. Arunachal Pradesh (Patkai Range, etc). Specimen record from Namdapha N.P. (Ghosh, 1987).

Remarks. Ellerman & Morrison-Scott (1951) included it as a subspecies of *Rattus bowersii*.

(182) **196. *Berylmys bowersii*** Bower's rat
Mus bowersii Anderson, 1879: 304. TYPE-LOCALITY: Hotha, Kakhyen Hills, W. Yunnan, China, 4500 ft.

Distribution & Status. Occurs mainly in the south bank of the Brahmaputra R., especially in e Arunachal Pradesh (Patkai Range, Mishmi Hills, etc). Mainly a montane species.

Subfamily ARVICOLINAE (Microtinae)

Voles

(183) **197. *Eothenomys melanogaster*** Père David's vole
Arvicola melanogaster Milne-Edwards, 1872a: 93 (footnote). TYPE-LOCALITY: Moupin, Sichuan, China.

Distribution & Status. Recorded at Dreyi in Mishmi Hills at 1550 m (5140 ft) elevation (Hinton, 1923a) and in Taley Valley W.S. at above 2000 m (Singh *et al.*, 1994). Status elsewhere is unclear.

Subspecies. 197a. *E. m. libonotus* Hinton, 1923a: 151. TYPE-LOCALITY: Dreyi, Mishmi Hills, Arunachal Pradesh (originally recorded as N. Assam), India, 5140 ft.

198. *Alticola roylei* Royle's high mountain vole
Arvicola roylei Gray, 1842: 265. TYPE-LOCALITY: Kumaon, Uttar Pradesh, India (Wroughton, Hinton).

Distribution & Status. Ghosh (1987) mentioned of its occurrence in Namdapha N.P., and Singh *et al.* (1994) in Tale Valley W.S. IUCN: LR (nt).

Subfamily RHIZOMYINAE

Bamboo rats

(184) **199. *Rhizomys pruinosus*** Hoary bamboo rat
R. pruinosus Blyth, 1851b: 519. TYPE-LOCALITY: Cherrapunji, Khasi Hills, Meghalaya, India.

Distribution & Status. Found in the hills and mountains, especially in E. Arunachal Pradesh. Recorded in Namdapha N.P.

Remarks. Corbet & Hill (1992) mentioned of its occurrence at altitudes from 1000 to 4000 m, however, in Meghalaya, specimens have been observed at 350 m elevation.

R. pruinosus

200. (185) ***Cannomys badius*** Bay bamboo rat, Lesser bamboo rat
Rhizomys badius Hodgson, 1841a: 60. TYPE-LOCALITY: Nepal.

Distribution & Status. Found all over, in the plains as well as hills.

Family HYSTRICIDAE

Old-world porcupines

(186) **201.** ***Hystrix brachyura*** Crestless Himalayan porcupine, Chinese porcupine
H. brachyura Linnaeus, 1758: 57. TYPE-LOCALITY: Malacca, Malaya.

Local Names. *Ketela pohu* (A), *Bobbi, Bîbu* (Adi), *Saba-chong* (Bugun), *Jûmpi* (Monpa), *Juimang* (Monpa, Zemithang area).

H. brachyura

Distribution & Status. Found all over, from plains to mountains. Not uncommon in the forest and near villages. The race *hodgsoni* is probably found in western Arunachal Pradesh while *subcristata* in the eastern areas, S. of the Brahmaputra R.

Subspecies. Three are generally recognised (van Weers, 1979), of which two occur in the area.
201a *H. b. hodgsoni*
Acanthion hodgsoni Gray, 1847b (June): 101. TYPE-LOCALITY: Nepal.
201b *H. b. subcristata*
H. subcristata Swinhoe, 1871: 638. TYPE-LOCALITY: Foochow, Fujian, China.

Remarks. Ellerman & Morrison-Scott (1951) treated it as *H. hodgsoni*. In many publications, it is often misidentified as Indian crested porcupine *H. indica* (Chatterjee, 1989; Singh *et al.*, 1994). *H. brachyura* is conspicuosly smaller in size than *indica* and has small, rudimentary or insignificant crest. IUCN: VU; WPA: Schedule II (I).

(187) **202. *Atherurus macrourus*** Asiatic brush-tailed porcupine
Hystrix macrourus Linnaeus, 1758: 57. TYPE-LOCALITY: Malacca, Malaya.

Local Names. *Kâkinimora, Ketela pohu* (A).

Distribution & Status. Rather uncommon. Occurs from plains to hills, especially in E. Arunachal Pradesh.

Subspecies. 202a *A. m. assamensis*
A. assamensis Thomas, 1921a: 598. TYPE-LOCALITY: Cherrapunji, Meghalaya, India.

Remarks. WPA: Schedule II (I). IUCN. EN.

Order LAGOMORPHA

Hares, Rabbits and Pikas

Formerly considered as rodents, the hares, rabbits and pikas are now classified as a clearly defined separate order—Lagomorpha. They differ from the rodents by their four incisors in the upper jaw against two, a large anterior pair and a smaller pair behind them. Other notable difference is in the testes which are permanently external. In case of rodents, these are retained in the abdomen except in the breeding season. Both the families, i.e., Leporidae and the Ochotonidae, are found in Arunachal Pradesh and are represented by two and one species respectively. The hares and rabbits have long ears and larger hind legs while the pikas have short ears and legs.

Family Leporidae

Hares

(188) **203. *Lepus nigricollis*** Indian hare, Rufous-tailed hare
L. nigricollis Cuvier, f., 1823: 307. TYPE-LOCALITY: Madras (Tamil Nadu), India.

Local Name. *Soha pohu* (A).

Distribution & Status. Common throughout including vicinity of human habitation. Occurs from plains to above 2000 m.

Subspecies. 203a *L. n. ruficaudatus* Rufous-tailed hare
L. ruficaudatus Geoffroy, I., 1826: 381. TYPE-LOCALITY: Bengal.

Remarks. *Lepus sadiya* Kloss, 1918: 95 (TYPE-LOCALITY: Kobo, *c.* 15 miles W. of Sadiya, Assam) have been synonymised with *L. nigricollis* (Corbet & Hill, 1992). Further study might recognise it at least as a subspecies. *L.nigricollis* is broadly sympatric with *Caprolagus hispidus* in the north bank of the Brahmaputra R.

The distribution in Assam and other areas of N.E. India not shown on the map in Corbet & Hill (1992). *L. nigricollis* is also known as the Black-naped hare, however, the subspecies *ruficaudatus* lacks the black on nape. WPA: Schedule IV.

(189) **204. *Caprolagus hispidus*** Hispid hare, Assam 'rabbit'
Lepus hispidus Pearson, in McClelland, 1839: 152. TYPE-LOCALITY: Himalayan foothills in N. Assam.

Local Name. *Khâgorikota pohu* (A).

Distribution & Status. Very rare. Found in the patches of *terai* grassland along the edge of the Himalayan foothills. Specific records from the banks of the Bor-Dikorai R. near Seijosa, Pakhui (Pakke) W.S. Also reported from D'Ering Memorial W.S. Other potential areas are the grassland along the Jia-Bhoreli, Nameri, Papum, Buroi, Borgang and Lohit rivers.

Remarks. CITES: Appendix I; IUCN: EN; WPA: Schedule I.

Family OCHOTONIDAE

Pikas or Mouse-hares

205. *Ochotona forresti* Forrest's pika, Steppe pika
Ochotona forresti Thomas 1923. 9, 11: 662. TYPE-LOCALITY: "N.W. flank [Likiang Range, 27° N., 100°30′ E.] 13,000' " [Yunnan, China].

Local Names. *Zabrang* (Monpa), *Breva jurdum* (Monpa, Zemithang area).

Distribution & Status. Status unclear, may be locally common. Observed in the high elevation areas (above 3000 m) of Tawang dist. Also reported from the high elevation areas of W. and E. Kameng. Anon (1997) reported of its occurrence in Tibet just N. of Dibang Valley dist in Medog area. Apparently occurs in other high elevation areas all along N. Arunachal Pradesh as its range extends up to Yunnan in S. China.

Remarks. Not found in present Assam (Arunachal Pradesh became a separate state in 1972). Ellerman & Morrison-Scott (1951) treated it as a subspecies of *O. pusilla*. Broadly sympatric with *O. roylei* and also perhaps *O. thibetana*. IUCN: LR (nt).

[***Ochotona thibetana*** Moupin pika
Lagomys thibetanus Milne-Edwards, in David, N., 1871: 93. TYPE-LOCALITY: Moupin, Sichuan, China.

Local Names. *Gumchi peechi* (Bhutia), *Zabrang* (Monpa), *Breva jurdum* (Monpa, Zemithang area).

Remarks. No specific record so far, however, most likely to occur all along the India-China border. Anon (1997) reported of its occurrence in Tibet just N. of Lohit dist in Zayu. IUCN: CR (ssp *sikimaria*)]

206. *Ochotona roylei* Royle's pika
Lagomys roylii Ogilby, 1839: LXIX, pl. 4. TYPE-LOCALITY: Choor mountain, 60 miles N. of Saharanpur, Himachal Pradesh (originally recorded as Punjab).

Local Names. *Zabrang* (Monpa), *Breva jurdum* (Monpa, Zemithang area).

Distribution & Status. Specific record from Mehao W.S. only (Chakraborty & Sen, 1991) and Dichu R.F., Lohit district (Singh *et al.*, 1995). However, its occurrence all along the Himalaya from Kashmir to N. Myanmar (Burma) and S. China indicates presence

Himalayan pika

across Arunachal Pradesh, especially along the India-China border. Usually they range between 3400 and 4300 m (Prater, 1948) but may come down in winter to up to 2400 m. At Mehao W.S., observed at as low as 1890 m.

Remarks. WPA: Schedule IV.

[***Ochotona himalayana*** Himalayan pika, Himalayan mouse-hare
O. himalayana Feng, 1973: 69, 73. TYPE-LOCALITY:'Qu-xiang, Bo-qu Valley, Nei-la-mu [= Nyalam] dist., alt. 3500 m' [Xigaze County, Tibet, China].

Remarks. Likely to occur in N. Arunachal Pradesh as Anon (1997) reported of its occurrence in Tibet just N. of Lohit dist. in Zayu. However, its status as a full species may still need confirmation through further study (Hoffmann, 1993). Earlier it was also considered a synonym of *O. roylei* (Corbet, 1978c; Weston, 1982).]

[***Ochotona curzoniae*** Curzon's pika
Lagomys curzoniae Hodgson, 1858: 207. TYPE-LOCALITY: Chumbi Valley, S. Tibetn, China.

Remarks. No specific record, however, likely to occur all along the India-China border in view of its distribution from Nepal to Sichuan. Anon (1997) reported of its occurrence in Tibet just N. of Tawang dist.

Earlier considered a subspecies of *O. dauurica* (Ellerman & Morrison-Scott, 1951; Mitchell, 1978). WPA: Schedule IV.]

Appendix 1

SPECIES NOT RECORDED BUT OCCUR IN THE ADJOINING AREAS

Order **Pholidota** Pangolins

Family **Manidae** Pangolins

1 *Manis crassicaudata* Indian pangolin

Order **Insectivora** Insectivores

Family **Talpidae** Moles

Subfamily Uropsilinae

2 *Uropsilus gracilis*

Subfamily Talpinae

3 *Scaptonyx fusicauda* Long-tailed mole

Family **Soricidae** Shrews

Subfamily Soricinae

4 *Blarinella quadraticauda* Sichuan short-tailed shrew

5 *Soriculus parca*

6 *Chimarrogale styani* Styan's water shrew

Order **Chiroptera** Bats

Suborder Microchiroptera

Family **Rhinopomatidae** Mouse-tailed bats

7 *Rhinopoma microphyllum* Greater mouse-tailed bat

Family **Rhinolophidae** Horseshoe bats

8 *Rhinolophus thomasi* Thomas's horseshoe bat

Family **Hipposideridae** Old-world leaf-nosed bats, Trident bats

9 *Coelops frithii* Tail-less leaf-nosed bat

Family **Vespertilionidae** Evening bats

Subfamily Vespertilioninae

10 *Myotis montivagus* Burmese whiskered bat

11 *Plecotus austriacus* Grey long-eared bat

12 *Eptesicus serotinus* Serotine

13 *Eptesicus gobiensis*

14 *Ia io* Great evening bat
15 *Pipistrellus joffrei* Joffre's pipistrelle
16 *Pipistrellus anthonyi*
17 *Pipistrellus circumdatus* Black gilded pipistrelle
18 *Philetor brachypterus*

Order **Primates** Primates
Suborder Anthropoidea
Family **Cercopithecidae** Old world monkeys
Subfamily Colobinae langur
19 *Presbytis cristatus* Silvered leaf monkey
20 *Presbytis geei* Golden langur, Golden leaf monkey

Order **Carnivora** Carnivores
Family **Felidae** Cats
21 *Felis manul* Pallas's cat
22 *Felis lynx* European lynx

Order **Artiodactyla** Even-toed ungulates
Family **Cervidae** Deer
Subfamily Cervinae
23 *Elaphodus cephalophus* Tufted deer
Family **Bovidae** Wild cattle, sheep and goats
24 *Hemitragus jemlahicus* Himalayan tahr

Order **Rodentia** Rodents
Family **Pteromyidae** Flying squirrels
25 *Trogopterus xanthipes* Complex-toothed flying squirrel
26 *Petinomys setosus* Temminck's flying squirrel
Family **Muridae** Rats and mice
Subfamily Murinae Rats and mice
27 *Diomys crumpi* Crump's mouse
28 *Niviventer confucianus*
Subfamily Arvicolinae (Microtinae) Voles
29 *Pitymys sikkimensis* Sikkim vole
Family **Ochotonidae** Pikas
30 *Ochotona gloveri*

Appendix 2

PROTECTED AREAS IN ARUNACHAL PRADESH (AREA IN KM^2)

National Parks

1. Mouling (Upper, West and East Siang districts) 483.00
2. Namdapha (Changlang dist.) 1985.23

Wildlife Sanctuaries

3. D'Ering Memorial (East Siang dist.) 190.00
4. Dibang (Dibang Valley dist.) 4149.00
5. Eaglenest (West Kameng dist.) 217.00
6. Itanagar (Papum Pare dist.) 140.30
7. Kamlang (Lohit dist.) 783.00
8. Kane (West Siang dist.) 55.00
9. Mehao (Dibang Valley dist.) 281.50
10. Pakke [Pakhui] (East Kameng dist.) 861.95
11. Sessa Orchid Sanctuary (West Kameng dist.) 100.00
12. Taley Valley (Lower Subansiri dist.) 337.00

Namdapha is also a Tiger Reserve under Project Tiger and is a proposed Biosphere Reserve.

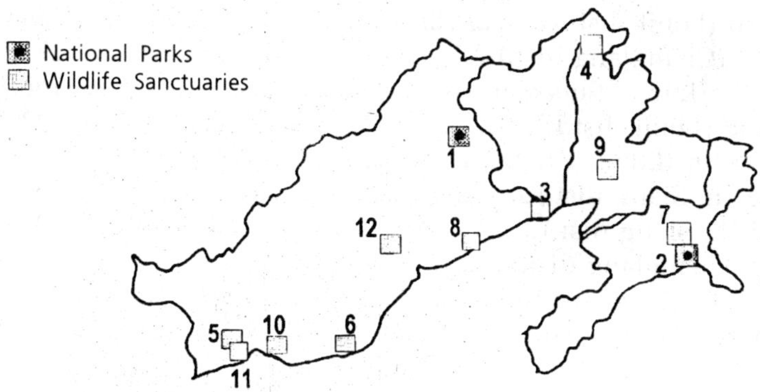

Protected areas

Appendix 3

MAIN RESERVED FORESTS

(AREA IN KM^2)

>400 km^2

1. Dichu (Lohit dist.) 1792.0
2. Papum (E. Kameng dist.) 1063.9
3. Kamlang (Lohit dist.) 680.0
4. Doimara (W. Kameng dist.) 534.1
5. Taley (Lower Subansiri dist.) .... 515.9 (incl. W.S.)
6. Tengapani (Lohit dist.) 443.9
7. Drupong (Papum Pare dist.) 420.8

200–399 km^2

8. Panir (Papum Pare & Lower Subansiri dists.) 389.8
9. Amortola (E. Kameng dist.) 294.2
10. Denning (Lohit dist.) 256.4

100–199 km^2

11. Tenga (W. Kameng dist.) 198.9
12. Dibang (Dibang Valley dist.) 197.9
13. Daporijo (Upper Subansiri dist.) 189.0
14. Digaru (Lohit dist.) 184.0
15. Diyun (Changlang dist.) 173.2
16. Kamala (Lower Subansiri dist.) 168.2
17. Turung (Lohit dist.) 143.5
18. Manabum (Lohit dist.) 136.1
19. Mebo (E. Siang dist.) 130.0
20. Remi (E. Siang dist.) 130.0
21. Miao (Changlang dist.) 125.8
22. Gutin (E. Siang dist.) 112.2
23. Namsang (Tirap dist.) 108.9

50–99 km²

24. Singen (Upper Subansiri dist.) 96.0
25. Pekom & Jeka (Upper Subansiri dist.) 78.0
26. Dipa (W. Siang dist.) 76.8
27. Honkap (Changlang dist.) 73.4
28. Pangsau (Changlang dist.) 69.1
29. Rima (Changlang dist.) 67.6
30. Paya (Lohit dist.) 66.0
31. Namphuk (Changlang dist.) 57.2
31. Tebang (Lohit dist.) 55.6
32. Deopani (Dibang Valley dist.) 54.6

Proposed Reserved Forests >300 km²

1. Delai (Lohit dist.) 1967.0
2. Hapoli (Lower Subansiri dist.) 380.7
3. Doimukh (Lower Subansiri dist.) 304.4

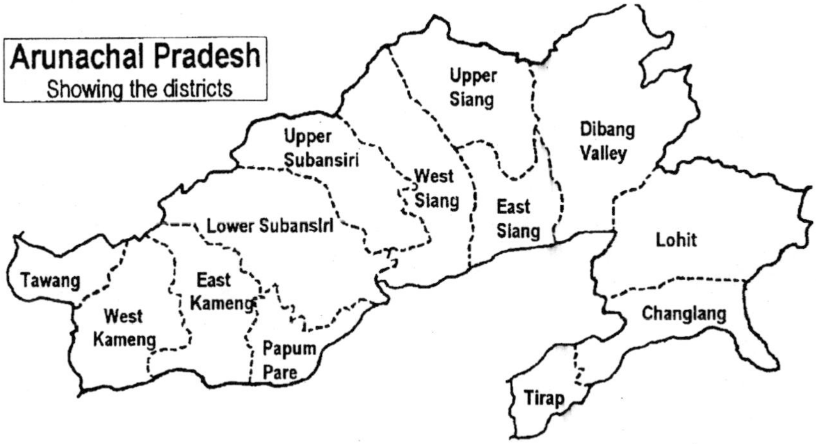

Two new districts have been created recently, Kurung Kamei (covering parts of Lower Subansiri) and Upper Dibang Valley.

BIBLIOGRAPHY

Abe, H. 1977. Variation and taxonomy of some small mammals from central Nepal. *J. Mammal soc. Japan* 7: 63–74.

Agrawal, V.C. 1975. Taxonomic study of the Indo-Burmese subspecies of the common tree-shrew, *Tupaia glis* Diard. pp. 385–394 in Tiwari, K.K. & Srivastava, C.B. (eds), *Dr. B.S. Chouhan commemoration volume* 1975. Zool. Soc. India, Orissa.

Agrawal, V.C. & Chakraborty, S. 1970. Occurrence of the woolly flying squirrel, *Eupe-taurus cinereus* ... In north sikkim. *J. Bombay Nat. Hist. Soc.* 66: 615–616.

Amato, G., Egan, M. & Rabinowitz, A. 1999. A new species of muntjac, *Muntiacus putaoensis* (Artiodactyla: Cervidae) from northern Myanmar. *Animal Conservation* 2: 1–7.

Anderson, J. 1877. Description of some new and little known Asiatic shrews ... *J. Asiatic soc. Bengal* 46, 2: 261–283.

—— 1879. *Anatomical and zoological researches: comprising an account of the two expeditions to western Yunnan.* Quaritch, 2 Vols., London.

—— 1881. *Catalogue of mammalia in the Indian museum, Calcutta.* Calcutta.

Anderson, K. 1911. Six new fruit-bats of the genera *Macroglossus* and *Syconycteris. Annals mag. Nat. Hist.* 7: 641–643.

—— 1918. Diagnoses of new bats of the families Rhinolophidae and Megadermatidae. *Annals Mag. Nat. Hist.* 2: 374–384.

Anderson, S. & Jones, J.K. (eds.). 1984. *Orders and families of recent mammals of the world.* Wiley, New York etc. 700pp.

Anon. 1997. *Distribution of mammalian species in China.* China Forestry Pub. House, Beijing.

Asakura, S. 1987. A note on a bear hybrid ... *International zoo yearbook.* 9: 88, 1pl.

Bailey, F. 1915. Notes from southern Tibet. *J. Bombay Nat. Hist. Soc.* 24: 72–78.

—— 1945. *China-Tibet-Assam.* Jonathan Cape, London.

Barrett-Hamilton, G.E.H. 1900. On geographical and individual variation in *Mus sylvaticus* and its allies. *Proceedings zool. Soc. Lond.*: 337–428, pl. XXV.

Bates, P.J. & Harrison, D.L. 1997. *Bats of the Indian Subcontinent.* Harrison Zoological Museum, Kent.

Bechstein, J.M. 1799, 1800. *Thomas pennant's allgemeine uebersicht der vierfussiger thiere.* Weimar.

Bennett, E.T. 1832. In: meeting of June 26, 1832. *Proc. Zool. Soc. Lond.* 121–127.

—— 1833. [meeting of June 11, 1833.] *Proceedings zool. Soc. Lond.* 68-69.

Benton, M.J. 1988. *The phylogeny and classification of tetrapods, Vol. 2: mammals.* Clarendon Press, Oxford. 344 pp.

Bhargava, R.N. 1988. The stump-tailed macaque in Arunachal Pradesh. *J. Bombay Nat. Hist. Soc.* 85: 182.

Blainville, H.M.D. De 1839–1864. *Osteographie, ou description iconographique des mammiferes* ... Paris (in 26 separately paginated parts).

Blanford, W.T. 1878. On some mammals from Tenasserim. *J. Asiatic soc. Bengal* 47, 2: 150–167.

—— 1888, 1891. *Fauna of British India includ. Ceylon & Burma. Mammalia,* part 1 (1888): 1–250; part 2 (1891): 251–617. Taylor & Francis, London.

Blyth, E. 1841. An amended list of the species of the genus. *Ovis. Proc. Zool. Soc. London* (1840): 62–79.

—— 1843. Memorandum from the Zoological Curator. *J. Asiatic Soc. Bengal* 12: 166–182.

—— 1844. Notices of various mammalia ... *J. Asiatic Soc. Bengal* 13: 463–494.

—— 1847. Supplementary report of the Curator. *J. Asiatic Soc. Bengal* 16: 728–737, 1pl.

—— 1848. Report of Curator ... *J. Asiatic Soc. Bengal* 17: 247–255.

—— 1850. Description of a new species of mole (*Talpa leucura,* Blyth). *J. Asiatic Soc. Bengal* 19: 215–217.

—— 1851a. Report on the mammalia ... Inhabiting Ceylon. *J. Asiatic Soc. Bengal* 20: 153–185.

—— 1851b. Notice of a collection of mammalia ... [from] Cherra punji in the Khasia Hills ... *J. Asiatic Soc. Bengal* 20: 517–524.

—— 1853. Report of the Curator, Zoological Department. *J. Asiatic Soc. Bengal* 22: 408–417.

—— 1854 (1853 ?). Report of Zoological Curator for September meeting. *J. Asiatic Soc. Bengal* 22: 589–594.

—— 1855. A memoir on the Indian species of shrews. *J. Asiatic Soc. Bengal* 24: 24–38.

Blyth, E. 1856. [report for October meeting, 1855] *J. Asiatic Soc. Bengal* 24: 711–723.

—— 1859. Report of the Curator. *J. Asiatic Soc. Bengal* 28: 271–298.

—— 1863. *Catalogue of the mammalia in the Museum Asiatic Society.* Calcutta, 187, XIII pp.

Boddaert, P. 1785. *Elenchus animalium* Vol 1. Hake, Rotterdam. 173pp.

Bonaparte, C.L. (J.L.). 1836–1841. *Iconografia della fauna Italica* fasc. I, xv. Rome.

Bonhote, J.L. 1901. On the squirrels of the *Sciurus erythraeus* group. *Annals Mag. Nat. Hist.* 7: 160–167.

Borang, A. & Thapliyal, G.S. 1993. Natural distribution and ecological status of non-human primates in Arunachal Pradesh. *Indian Forester* 119 (1): 834–844.

Brookes, J. 1828. *A catalogue of the anatomical and zoological museum of J. Brookes ... Pt.* 1. London, 76pp.

Brünnich, M.T. 1782. *Dyrenes historie og dyre-samlingen udi universetets natur-theater. Band* 1. Kobenhavn.

Buchannan, F. 1800. Description of the *Vespertilio plicatus. Transactions Linn. Soc. Lond* 5: 261–263, 1pl.

Buckland, F. 1872. A new rhinoceros at the zoological gardens. *Land & Water* 1872, 2: 89.

Butler, P.M. 1988. Phylogeny of the insectivores. pp. 117–141 in Benton, M.J. (*q.v.*).

Cabrera, A. 1925. *Genera mammalium. Insectivora, galeopithecia.* Madrid.

Cai, G-Q. & Zhang, N.-Z. 1980. On new subspecies of Blanford's fruit bat and the orange-bellied himalayan squirrel from Xizang. *Acta Zootaxon. Sin.* 5: 443–446.

Campbell, C.B.G. 1974. On the phyletic relationships of the tree shrews. *Mammal Review* 4: 125–143.

Cantor, T. 1846. Catalogue of mammalia inhabiting the Malayan peninsula and islands ... *J. Asiatic Soc. Bengal* 15: 171–203.

Catton, C. 1990. *Pandas.* Christopher Helm, London.

Chakraborty, S. 1975. On a collection of mammals from Bhutan. *Rec. Zool. Surv. India* 68: 1–20.

Chakraborty, S. & Sen, A.K. 1991. Mammals of the Mehao wildlife sanctuary (Dibang valley district, Arunachal Pradesh) with remarks on their status. *Rec. Zool. Surv. India* 88 (3 & 4): 263–285.

Champion, H. & Seth, S.K. 1964. A revised survey of the forest types of India. Forest Research Institutes & Colleges, Dehra Dun.

Chasen, F.N. 1940. A handlist of Malaysian mammals. *Bulletin Raffles Mus.* 15: 209pp.

Chatterjee, A.K. 1989. Survey of snow leopard and associated animals in Mouling national park, East Siang district, Arunachal Pradesh. *Arunachal Forest News* 7 (1 & 2): 10–15.

Chatterjee, A.K. & Chandiramani, S.S. 1986. An introduction to Namdapha tiger reserve, Arunachal Pradesh, India. *Tigerpaper* 12 (13): 22–27.

Chaturvedi, Y. 1969. Two new records of bats from Assam and Andaman Is. *Labdev* 7B: 74–75.

Choudhury, A. U. 1985. Distribution of Indian one-horned rhinoceros. *Tigerpaper* XII (2): 25–30.

—— 1986a. Discovery of Phayre's leaf monkey in Assam. *The Sentinel*, August 31, Guwahati.

—— 1986b. Wildlife in north-east India. *North-eastern Geographer* 18 (1 & 2): 92–101 (pub. in 1987).

—— 1987a. Notes on the distribution and conservation of Phayre's leaf monkey and hoolock gibbon in India. *Tigerpaper* XIV (2): 2–6.

—— 1987b. Railway threat to Kaziranga. *Oryx* 21: 160–163.

—— 1988a. Priority ratings for conservation of Indian primates. *Oryx* 22: 89–94.

—— 1988b. Conservation in Manas tiger reserve. *Tigerpaper* XV (2): 23–27.

—— 1988c. Phayre's leaf monkey (*T. phayrei*) in Cachar. *J. Bombay Nat. Hist. Soc.* 85(3): 485–492.

—— 1988d. A primate survey in southern Assam, India. *Primate conservation* 9: 123–125.

—— 1989a. Ecology of the capped langur in Assam, India. *Folia Primatologica*, 52: 88–92.

—— 1989b. Tigers in India today. *Tigerpaper* XVI (3): 1–6.

—— 1989c. Vocalisation in hoolock gibbon. *Primate Report* 25: 53–54.

—— 1989d. Pabitora, Assam's rhino reserve. *The India Magazine* 9: 46–54.

—— 1989e. On the distribution of Asian horseshoe bat. *J. Bombay Nat. Hist. Soc.* 86 (3): 436

—— 1989f. Primates of Assam: their distribution, habitat and status. Ph. D. Thesis, Gauhati University, Guwahati. 300pp + maps.

—— 1990a. Overlapping distribution of capped langur and Phayre's leaf monkey. *J. Bombay Nat. Hist. Soc.* 87(1): 8.

—— 1990b. Some observations on the behaviour of capped langur in Assam, India. *Tigerpaper* XVII (1): 23–26.

Choudhury, A. U. 1990c. Population dynamics of hoolock gibbons in Assam, India. *American J. Primatol.* 20: 37–41.

—— 1990d. Primates in Bhutan. *Oryx* 24: 125.

—— 1991a. Stumptailed macaque *Macaca arctoides* in Manipur. *J. Bombay Nat. Hist. Soc.* 88 (1): 114.

—— 1991b. In search of the silvered leaf. *Hornbill* 1: 28–31.

—— 1991c. Ecology of the hoolock gibbon, a lesser ape in the tropical forests of N.E. India. *J. Tropical Ecology* 7: 147–153.

—— 1991d. Status of wild elephants in Cachar and North Cachar Hills, Assam—a preliminary survey. *J. Bombay Nat. Hist. Soc.* 88 (2): 215–221.

—— 1991e. Indian rhino, what's that ? *The Telegraph Color Mag.* 27 october, 6–10pp.

—— 1992a. The slow loris (*Nycticebus coucang*) in north-east India. *Primate Report* 34: 77–83.

—— 1992b. Golden langur-distribution confusion. *Oryx* 26: 172–173.

—— 1992c. On probable sympatric distribution of *Presbytis geei* and *P. pileatus* in Bhutan. *J. Ecological Soc.* 5: 49–51.

—— 1992d. Wildlife in Manipur—a preliminary survey. *Tigerpaper* XIX (1): 20–28.

—— 1993a. The clouded leopard in Assam. *Oryx* 27: 51–53.

—— 1993b. Letters. *Hornbill* 1993 (2): 18–19.

—— 1993c. *A naturalist in Karbi Anglong*. Gibbon Books, Guwahati. 78pp, maps, pl.

—— 1994a. *Checklist of the mammals of Assam*. Gibbon Books, Guwahati. 59pp.

—— 1994b. The decline of the wild water buffalo in northeastern India. *Oryx* 28 (1): 70–73.

—— 1994c. Wild buffalo *Bubalus bubalis* in Dhakuakhana, Lakhimpur district of Assam. *J. Bombay Nat. Hist. Soc.* 91 (1): 139.

—— 1994d. Further observations on Phayre's leaf monkey (*T. phayrei)* in Cachar, Assam. *J. Bombay Nat. Hist. Soc.* 91 (2): 203–210.

—— 1994e. The wildlife of Dibrugarh district. *Souvenir-Dibrugarh'* 94. pp. 13–15.

—— 1994f. Phayre's leaf monkey in northeastern India. *Tigerpaper* XXI (3): 1–4.

—— 1994g. A report on bird survey in Dibru-Saikhowa wildlife sanctuary, Assam, India. Report to OBC, UK. 71pp + maps.

—— 1995a. The primates of Namdapha national park. *IPPL News* 22 (2): 23–24.

Choudhury, A.U. 1995b. *Wildlife survey in Bherjan, Borajan & Podumoni RFs of Tinsukia district, Assam, with a proposal for a wildlife sanctuary*. The Rhino Foundation for nat. in N.E. India, Guwahati. 18pp (with maps).

—— 1995c. Mammals of southern districts of Assam. *Cheetal*, 34 (2): 10–17.

—— 1995d. Status of wild elephants in Dibang Valley of Arunachal Pradesh. *J. Bombay Nat. Hist. Soc.* 92 (3): 417.

—— 1996a. A survey of hoolock gibbon (*Hylobates hoolock*) in southern Assam, India. *Primate Report* 44: 77–85.

—— 1996b. Red panda in Garo Hills. *Environ* IV (i): 21.

—— 1996c. The greater one-horned rhino outside the protected areas in Assam, India. *Pachyderm* 22: 7–9.

—— 1996d. Survey of primates in some parts of eastern and central Assam. Final Report to ASTEC (Assam,Science, Technology & Environment Council), Guwahati. 32pp, maps.

—— 1996e. Primates in Assam—status and conservation. *Tigerpaper* XXIII (3): 14–17.

—— 1996f. The marbled cat *Felis marmorata* Martin in Assam-some recent records. *J. Bombay Nat. Hist. Soc.* 93: 583–584.

—— 1996g. The clouded leopard. *Cheetal* 35 (1–2): 13–18.

—— 1996h. Trekking through Kamlang. *Sanctuary Asia* XVI (5): 44–49.

—— 1997a. Mammals of Namcha Barwa, Tibet. *Oryx* 31 (2): 91–92.

—— 1997b. The status of the Sumatran rhinoceros in north-eastern India. *Oryx* 31 (2): 151–152.

—— 1997c. White-tailed mole *Talpa micrura leucura* Blyth in Assam-some new records. *J. Bombay Nat. Hist. Soc.* 94: 145.

—— 1997d. The status of bears in Assam, India. *International Bear News* 6 (2): 16.

—— 1997e. *Checklist of the mammals of Assam*. Revised 2nd edn. Gibbon Books & ASTEC, Guwahati. 103pp.

—— 1997f. Small carnivores (mustelids, viverrids, herpestids, and one ailurid) in Arunachal Pradesh, India. *Small Carnivore Conservation* 17: 7–9.

—— 1997g. Red panda *Ailurus fulgens* F. Cuvier in the north-east with an important record from Garo Hills. *J. Bombay Nat. Hist. Soc.* 94 (1): 145–147.

—— 1997h. Indian one-horned rhinoceros *Rhinoceros unicornis* Linnaeus 1758, in Arunachal Pradesh. *J. Bombay Nat. Hist. Soc.* 94 (1): 152–153.

—— 1998a. Wild water buffalo *Bubalus bubalis/arnee* in Dibang Valley district of Arunachal Pradesh. *J. Bombay Nat. Hist. Soc.* 95 (1): 110–112.

Choudhury, A.U. 1998b. Père David's macaque discovered in India. *The Rhino Foundation* ...N.E. *India Newsletter* 2 (1): 7.

—— 1999a. Status and Conservation of the Asian elephant *Elephas maximus* in north-eastern India. *Mammal Review* 29 (3): 141–173.

—— 1999b. Status of the wild water buffalo *Bubalus arnee* in Lohit district, Arunachal Pradesh. *J. Bombay Nat. Hist. Soc.* 96 (1): 130–132.

—— 1999c. The gaur *Bos gaurus* in Dibang Valley district of Arunachal Pradesh. *J. Bombay Nat. Hist. Soc.* 96 (2): 311–313.

—— 1999d. Mustelids, Viverrids and Herpestids of Northeastern India. *ENVIS Bull: Wildlife and Protected Areas* 2 (2): 43–47.

—— 2000. *Panthera tigris* in North East India. In *Royal Bengal Tiger in the 21st Century*. pp. 61–77. Vision Publications Pvt. Ltd (on behalf of Nature Environment & Wildlife Society), Calcutta.

—— 2001. An overview of the status and conservation of the red panda *Ailurus fulgens* in India, with reference to its global status. *Oryx* 35 (3): 250–259.

—— 2002a. *Petaurista nobilis singhei*—first record in India and a note on its taxonomy. *J. Bombay Nat. Hist. Soc.* 99 (1): 30–34.

—— 2002b. Possible occurrence of Tibet red deer *Cervus elaphus wallichi* in Arunachal Pradesh. *J. Bombay Nat. Hist. Soc.* 99 (2): 286–288.

—— 2002c. Distribution and conservation of the Gaur *Bos gaurus* in the Indian Subcontinent. *Mammal Review* 32 (3): 199–226.

—— 2002d. Status and conservation of the stump-tailed macaque *M. arctoides* in India. *Primate Report*. 63: 63–72.

—— 2002e. Biodiversity survey in the upper areas of East Kameng district, Arunachal Pradesh. Interim report. WWF-India Assam & Arunachal Office, Guwahati. 12pp, plate.

Cooper, H. 1923. The Mishmi takin (*Budorcas taxicolor*). *J. Bombay Nat. Hist. Soc.* 29: 550–551.

Corbet, G.B. 1978. *The mammals of the Palaearctic Region*. British Museum (Natural History), London.

Corbet, G.B. & Clutton-Brock, J. 1984. Appendix: Taxonomy and Nomenclature. pp. 434–438 in Mason, I. L. (ed.) *Evolution of domesticated animals*. Longman, London.

Corbet, G.B. & Hill, J.E. 1992. *The mammals of the Indomalayan Region: a systematic review*. Oxford Univ. Press, Oxford.

Collar, N.J., Crosby, M.J. & Stattersfield, A. J. 1994. *Birds to watch 2, the world list of threatened birds*. Birdlife International, Cambridge.

Cretzschmar, J. 1826–1831. Saugethiere, pp. 1–78 in *Atlas zu der reise im Nordlichen Afrika von Edouard Ruppell*. Frankfurt.

Cubitt, G. & Mountfort, G. 1985. *Wild India.* Collins, London.

Cuvier, F. 1822. Du genre paradoxure et de deux especes nouvelles ... *Memoires Mus. Hist. Nat. Paris* 9: 41–48, pl. 4.

—— 1823. Lievre, *Lepus.* 26: 299–316; Loutre, *Lutra.* 27: 237–250. *Dictionnaire des Sciences Naturelle.* Strasbourg & Paris.

—— 1825. In *histoire naturelle des mammiferes, avec des figures originales, etc.*, Ed. e. Geoffroy st. Hilaire and f. Cuvier. Paris.

Cuvier, G. 1823–24. *Recherches sur les ossemens fossile* ... Paris.

Dào Van Tiên & Cao Van Sung. 1990. Six new Vietnamese rodents. *Mammalia* 54: 233–238.

Das, P.K. 1986. Studies on the taxonomy ... of bats obtained by the Silent Valley (Kerala) expedition, 1980. *Records Zool. Surv. India* 8: 259–276.

Desmarest, A.G. 1817. Civette, Vol. 7: 159–171; dauphin, *Delphinus,* Vol. 9: 146–179; ecureuil, Vol. 10: 94–111, in *Nouveau Dictionnaire D'Histoire Naturelle* ... Paris.

—— 1820. *Mammalogie ou descroption des espece de mammiferes. In: Encyclopedie methodique* ... part 1. Agasse, Paris.

—— 1822. *Ibid,* part 2: 277–555.

Dey, S. 1995. New site confirmed for clouded leopard—a globally threatened species. *Arunachal Forest News* 13 (1 & 2): 37–3.

Diard, P.M. 1820. [Report of a meeting on Mar. 10th] *Asiatic J. Month. Reg.* 10: 472–478 ? (*n.v.*).

Dobson, G.E. 1871a. On some new species of Malayan bats ... *Proceedings Asiatic Soc. Bengal*: 105–106.

—— 1871b. Description of four new species of Malayan bats ... *J. Asiatic Soc. Bengal* 40: 260–267, 2pls.

—— 1871c. Notes on nine species of Indian and Indo-Chinese Vespertilionidae ... *Proceedings Asiatic. Soc. Bengal*: 210–215.

—— 1872a. Brief descriptions of five new species of Rhinolophine bats. *J. Asiatic Soc. Bengal* 41: 336–338.

—— 1872b. Note on some bats... In the northwestern Himalaya. *Proceedings Asiatic Soc. Bengal:* 208–210.

—— 1872c. pp. 220–223 in Stoliczka, F. 1872 (*q.v.*).

—— 1874. List of chiroptera inhabiting the Khasia Hills ... *J. Asiatic Soc. Bengal* 43, 2: 234–236.

—— 1875. On the genus *Scotophilus* ... *Proceedings Zool. Soc. Lond.*: 368–373.

—— 1876. *Monograph of the Asiatic chiroptera and catalogue of the species of bats in the collection of the Indian Museum, Calcutta,* Calcutta, London.

Dufresne, C. 1797. Sur une nouvelle espece de singe. *Bulletin Soc. Philom. Paris* 1, 7: 49.

Dutta, A.K. 1991. *Unicornis. The great Indian one-horned rhino.* Konark pub., Delhi.

Ellerman, J.R. & Morrison-Scott, T.C.S. 1951. *Checklist of Palaearctic and Indian mammals,* 1758 to 1946. British Museum (natural history) (2nd ed., 1966), London.

Elliot, W. 1839. A catalogue of the species of mammalia found in the southern Mahratta country ... *Madras J. Litt. Sci.* 10: 92–108, 205–233, 1 pl.

Erxleben, J.C.P. 1777. *Systema regni animales .. Classis i. Mammalia.* Lipsia: XLVIII, 636pp.

Finn, F. 1929. *Sterndale's mammalia of India.* Revised edn. Thacker, Spink, Calcutta & Simla.

Fischer, G. 1804. *Anatomie der maki, und der ihnen verwandten thiere.* Andreaische Buchhdl., Frankfurt. XXIV, 194pp.

—— 1814. *Zoognosia tabulis synopticis illustrata* Vol. 3, 732pp. Vsevolozsky, Moscow.

Flynn, J.J. et al. 1988. Phylogeny of the carnivora. pp.73–116 in Benton, M.J., 1988b (*q.v.*).

Fooden, J. 1975. Taxonomy and evolution of liontail and pigtail macaques. *Fieldiana Zoology* 67: 169pp.

—— 1976. Primates obtained in peninsular Thailand, June–July, 1973, with notes on the distribution of continental southeast Asian leaf-monkeys (*Presbytis*). *Primates* (Inuyama), 17(1): 95–118.

—— 1982. Taxonomy and evolution of the sinica group of macaques: 3. Species and subspecies accounts of *Macaca assamensis. Fieldiana Zoology.* N.s. 10: 1–52.

—— 1983. Taxonomy and evolution of the sinica group of macaques: 4. Species account of *Macaca thibetana. Fieldiana Zoology.* N.s. 17: 20pp.

—— 1986. Taxonomy and evolution of the sinica group of macaques: 5. Overview of natural history. *Fieldiana Zoology.* N.s. 29: 1–22.

—— 1988. Taxonomy and evolution of the sinica group of macaques: 6. Interspecific comparison and synthesis. *Fieldiana Zoology.* N.s. 45: 1–44.

—— 1990. The bear macaques, *Macaca arctoides ... J. Human Evol.* 19: 607–686.

Fooden, J., Quan Guoqiang, Wang Zongren, & Wang Yingxiang. 1985. The stumptail macaques of China. *American J. Primatol.* 8: 11–30.

Francis, C.M. & Hill, J.E. 1986. A review of the Bornean *Pipistrellus* ... *Mammalia* 50: 43–55.

Gee, E.P. 1956. A new species of langur in Assam. *J. Bombay Nat. Hist. Soc.* 53: 252–254.

—— 1961. The distribution and feeding habits of the golden langur, *Presbytis geei* Gee (Khajuria, 1956). *J. Bombay Nat. Hist. Soc.* 58: 1–12.

—— 1964. *The wild life of India*. Collins, London.

—— 1967a. Occurrence of the nayan or great Tibetan sheep, *Ovis ammon hodgsoni* Blyth in Bhutan. *J. Bombay Nat. Hist. Soc.* 64: 553.

—— 1967b. Occurrence of brown bear, *Ursus arctos* Linnaeus, in Bhutan. *J. Bombay Nat. Hist. Soc.* 64: 551–552.

Geoffroy, (-Saint Hilaire), E. 1810. Sur les phyllostomes et les megadermes ... *Annales Mus. Hist. Nat. Paris* 15: 157–198, 3pls.

—— 1818. *Description de l'egypte ... Description des mammiferes*. 2. Paris.

Geoffroy, (-Saint Hilaire), E. & Cuvier, G. 1819–1842. *Histoire naturelle des mammiferes* ... Paris (many names usually attributed to this are invalid since they were not allocated to a genus).

Geoffroy, (-Saint Hilaire), I. 1826. Lievre *Lepus*. pp. 378–387 in Bory de Saint Vincent (ed.) *Dictionnaire classique d'histoire naturelles* ... Vol. 9.

—— 1831–1834. Mammiferes, in Belanger, C., *Voyage aux indes-orientales* ... Bertrand, Paris.

Ghosh, A.K. 1987. *Qualitative analysis of faunal resources of proposed Namdapha biosphere reserve, Arunachal Pradesh*. Zoological Survey of India, Calcutta.

Ghosh, A.K. & Biswas, B. 1976. A note on the ecology of golden langurs: *Presbytis geei* Khajuria. *J. Bombay Nat. Hist. Soc.* 72: 524–527.

Ghose, R.K. & Saha, S.S. 1981. Taxonomic review of Hodgson's giant flying squirrel, *Petaurista magnificus* ..., with description of a new subspecies from Darjeeling dist, W. Bengal, India. *J. Bombay Nat. Hist. Soc.* 78: 93–102.

Gill, T. 1875. Synopsis of insectivorous mammals. *Bulletin US Geol. Geogr. Surv. Territ.* 2(2): 91–120.

Gittelman, J.L. (ed.). 1989. *Carnivore behaviour, ecology and evolution*. Cornell U.P., Ithaca.

Glatston, A.R. (ed.). 1989. *Red panda biology*. SPB Academic Publishing, Hague., 187pp.

Gogoi, P.C. 1986. *Rahashyamoi banyaprani.* 2nd eds. Datta Baruah & Co., Guwahati (in assamese).

Gray, A.P. 1972. *Mammalian hybrids: a check-list with bibliography.* Commonwealth Agricultural Bureaux, Slough. 262pp.

Gray, J.E. 1830–1835. *Illustrations of Indian zoology chiefly selected from the collection of Major-General Hardwicke, FRS.* London.

—— 1831. [Exhibition of mammalia] *Proceedings Zool. Soc. Lond.*: 94–96.

—— 1832. [Specimens and drawings of numerous animals referable to the genus *Paradoxurus*] *Proceedings Zool. Soc. Lond.*: 63–68.

—— 1837. Description of some new and little known mammalia ... *Magazine Nat. Hist.* 1: 577–587.

—— 1838. A revision of the genera of bats ... *Magazine Zool. Bot.* 2: 483–505.

—— 1842. Description of some new genera and fifty unrecorded species of mammalia. *Annals. Mag. Nat. Hist.* 10: 255–267.

—— 1846. New species of mammalia. *Annals Mag. Nat. Hist.* 18: 211–212.

—— [1847]a. *Catalogue of the specimens of mammalia and birds of Nepal and Thibet presented by B. H. Hodgson* ... British Museum, London. (dated 1846, published Jan. 1847.).

—— 1847b. On the porcupines of the older or eastern continent. *Proceedings Zool. Soc. Lond.* 15: 97–104.

—— 1853. Observations on some rare indian animals. *Proceedings Zool. Soc. Lond.*: 190–192, pls. 35–38.

—— 1863.... *Proceedings Zool. Soc. Lond.*: 94.

—— 1865. Revision of the genera and species of mustelidae ... *Proceedings Zool. Soc. Lond.*: 100–154, pl. 7.

Griffith, E. 1821. *General and particular descriptions of the vertebrated animals* ... London. 143pp.

Groves, C.P. 1967.Geographic variation in the hoolock or white-browed gibbon (*Hylobates hoolock*). *Folia Primatologica,* 7: 276–283.

—— 1972. Systematics and phylogeny of gibbons, in *gibbon and siamang,* i., Ed. D.M.Rumbaugh, pp. 1–89. S.Karger, Basel.

—— 1975. The taxonomy of the genus *Moschus* (Mammalia, Artiodactyla), with particular reference to the Indian region. *J. Bombay Nat. Hist. Soc.* 72: 262–276.

—— 1981. Ancestors for the pigs: taxonomy and phylogeny of the genus *Sus. Technical Bull., Dept. Prehist., Res. Sch. Pacific stud., Aust. Nat. Univ.* 3: 96pp.

Groves, C.P. 1982. Geographical variation in the barasingha or swamp deer (*Cervus duvauceli*). *J. Bombay Nat. Hist. Soc.* 79: 620–629.

—— 1989. *A theory of human and primate evolution*. Clarendon Press, Oxford. 388pp.

Groves, C.P. & Grubb, P. 1985. Reclassification of the serows and gorals ... pp. 45–50 in Lovari, S. (ed.) *The biology and management of mountain ungulates*. Croom Helm, Beckenham.

—— 1987. Relationships of living Cervidae. pp. 21–59 in Wemmer, C.M. (ed.) *Biology and management of the cervidae*. Smithsonian Institute, Washington.

Groves, C.P., Yingxiang, W. & Grubb, P. 1995. Taxonomy of musk deer, genus *Moschus* (Moschidae, Mammalia). *Acta Theriologica Sinica* 15(3): 181–197.

Gueldenstaedt, A.L. 1776. Chaus, animal feli affine descriptum. *Novi Comment. Acad. Sci. Imp. Petropol.* 20: 483–500, pls. 14,15.

Gureev, A.A. 1979. [*Fauna SSSR / mammals*] IV (2) *insectivora*. Nauka, Leningrad. 502pp.

Haimoff, E.H. 1985. Some observations on the singing behaviour of the hoolock gibbon (*H. hoolock*). *J. Bombay Nat. Hist. Soc.* 82: 1–12.

Hamilton-Smith, C. 1827. The carnassiers (Vol. 2); order VII-Ruminantia (Pecora, Lin.). (Vol. 4: 1–428; Vol. 5: 296–376) in Griffith, E. *et al., Cuvier's animal kingdom.*

synopsis of the species of the class mammalia. Whittaker, London.

Hardwicke, T. 1825a. Descriptions of two species of antelope from India. *Transactions Linn. Soc. Lond.* 14: 518–524.

—— 1825b. Description of a new species of tailed bat (*Taphozous*) found in Calcutta. *Transactions Linn. Soc. Lond.* 14: 525–526.

Harlan, R. 1831. Description of a new species of orang (*Simia hoolock*) from the north-eastern province of British East India, lately the kingdom of Assam. *Transactions Am. Phil. Soc.* 4,1: 52–59, pl. 2.

Harper, F. 1940. The nomemclature and type localities of certain old world mammals. *J. Mammal* 21: 191–203; 322–332.

Hayman, R.W. 1961. The red goral of the north-east frontier region. *Proc. Zool. Soc. London* 136: 317–324.

Henri D'Orléans. 1898. *Prince: du Tonkin aux Indes, Janvier 1895-Janvier 1896.* Calmann Lêvy, Paris.

Heptner, V.G. & Sludskii, A.A. 1992. Mammals of the Soviet Union. Vol. II, part 2. English translation.Originally published in 1972 in Russian. Amerind Pub. Co., New Delhi.

Heude, P.M. 1901. Notes sur quelques ursides ... etc. *Memoires Hist. Nat. Emp. Chin.* 5(1): 1–43, pls I–XI.

Hill, J.E. 1974. A new family, genus and species of bat ... From Thailand. *Bulletin Br. Mus. Nat. Hist.* (zool.) 27: 127–138.

—— 1983. Bats ... From Indo-Australia. *Bulletin Br. Mus. Nat. Hist.* (Zool.) 45: 103–208.

—— 1986. A note on *Rhinolophus pearsonii* ... and *Rhinolophus yunanensis* ... *J. Bombay Nat. Hist. Soc.* 83 (suppl.): 12–18.

Hill, J.E. & Thonglongya, K. 1972. Bats from Thailand and Cambodia. *Bulletin Br. Mus. Nat. Hist.* (*Zool.*) 22: 171–196.

Hill, J.E. *et al.* 1986. The taxonomy of leaf-nosed bats of the *Hipposideros bicolor* Group ... *Mammalia* 50: 535–540.

Hill, W..C.O. 1939. A new leaf-monkey hybrid ... *Spolia Zeylan.* 21: 265–275, pls 32, 33.

Hill, W..C.O. & Bernstein, I.S. 1969. On the morphology, behaviour and systematic status of Assam macaque *Macaca assamensis. Primates* (Iinuyama) 10: 1–17.

Hinton, M.A.C. 1918. Report on the house rats of India, Burma, and Ceylon [part 1]. *J. Bombay Nat. Hist. Soc.* 26: 59–88.

—— 1919. Ditto, parts 2 and 3. *J. Bombay Nat. Hist. Soc.* 26: 384–416; 716–725.

—— 1923a. On the voles collected by Mr. G. Forrest in Yunnan ... *Annals Mag. Nat. Hist.* 11: 145–162.

—— 1923b. On the capped langurs (*Pithecus pileatus* Blyth and its allies). *Annals. Mag. Nat. Hist.* 29: 77–83.

—— 1923c. Scientific results from the mammal survey no. XXXVI: on capped langurs (*Pithecus pileatus,* Blyth and its allies). *J. Bombay Nat. Hist. Soc.* 29: 77–83.

Hinton, M.A.C. & Lindsay, H.M. 1926. Report No. 41: Assam and Mishmi Hills. Bombay Natural History Society's mammal survey of India, Burma and Ceylon. *J. Bombay Nat. Hist. Soc.* 31: 383403.

Hodgson, B.H. 1831. Contributions in natural history. *Gleanings Sci.* 3: 320–324, pl. XXI.

—— 1833a. Description of the wild dog of the Himalaya. *Asiatic Res.* 18, 2: 221–237, 3pls.

—— 1833b. The wild goat and the wild sheep of Nepal. *Asiatic Res.* 18, 2: 129–138, 3pls.

—— 1835a. Synopsis of the vespertilionidae of Nipal. *J. Asiatic Soc. Bengal* 4: 699–701.

—— 1835b. Description of the little musteline animals, denominated Kathiah nyul ... *J. Asiatic Soc. Bengal* 4: 702–704.

Hodgson, B.H. 1836. Synoptical description of sundry new animals ... *J. Asiatic Soc. Bengal* 5: 231–238.

—— 1839a. On three new species of musk (*Moschus*)... *J. Asiatic Soc. Bengal* 8: 202–203.

—— 1839b. Summary description of four new species of otter. *J. Asiatic Soc. Bengal* 8: 319–320.

—— 1841a. New species of *Rhizomys* discovered in Nepal. *Calcutta J. Nat. Hist.* 2: 60–61.

—— 1841b. Classified catalogue of mammals of Nepal ... *Calcutta J. Nat. Hist.* 2: 212–221.

—— 1841c. On a new species of *Prionodon, P. pardicotor nobis. Calcutta J. Nat. Hist.* 2: 57–60, pl. 1.

—— 1841d. Three new species of monkey ... *J. Asiatic Soc. Bengal* 9 (1840): 1211–1213.

—— 1841e ... *J. Asiatic Soc. Bengal* 10: 721, 777.

—— 1845. On the rats, mice, and shrews of the central region of Nepal. *Annals Mag. Nat. Hist.* 15: 266–270.

—— 1847a. On a new form of the hog kind or suidae. *J. Asiatic Soc. Bengal* 16: 423–428, pls. XII, XIII.

—— 1847b. On a new species of *Plecotus. J. Asiatic Soc. Bengal* 16: 894–896.

—— 1847c. ... *J. Asiatic Soc. Bengal* 16: 763.

—— 1850. On the takin of the eastern Himalaya ... *J. Asiatic Soc.bengal* 19:65–75, pls. 1–3.

Hoffmann, R.S. 1986. A review of the genus *Soriculus* ... *J. Bombay Nat. Hist. Soc.* 82: 459–481.

Hohmann, G. 1988. Analysis of loud calls provides new evidence for hybridization between two Asian leaf monkeys (*Presbytis johnii, P. entellus). Folia Primatol.* 51: 209–213.

Horsfield, T. 1821–1824. *Zoological researches in Java* ... Kingbury, Parbury & Allen.,London.

—— 1825. Description of the *Helarctos euryspilus* ... *Zoological J. Lond.* 2: 221–234.

—— 1831. Observations on two species of bats, from Madras ... *Proceedings Zool. Soc. Lond.*: 113–114.

—— 1840. List of mammalia and birds collected in Assam ... *Proceedings Zool. Soc. Lond.* (1839): 146–167.

—— 1851. *A catalogue of the mammalia in the Museum of the East India Company*. London. 212pp.

—— 1855. Brief notices of ... Mammalia ... in Nepal. *Annals. Mag. Nat. Hist.*16: 101–114.

Husson, A.M. 1955. Note on the cotypes of *Vespertilio harpia* Temminck, 1840 ... *Zoologische Meded. Leiden* 33: 121–125.

Illiger, C. 1815. Ueberblick der saugethiere ... *Abhandlungen Preuss. Akad. Wiss.* (1804–1811): 39–159.

Inglis, C.M., Travers, W.L., O'Donel, H.V. & Shebbeare, E.O. 1919. A tentative list of the vertebrates of the Jalpaiguri district, Bengal. *J. Bombay Nat. Hist. Soc.* 26: 819–825.

IUCN. 2002. *2002 IUCN Red List of threatened animals.* IUCN, Gland, Switzerland.

Jaeger, J.-J. 1988. Rodent phylogeny: new data and old problems. pp. 177–199 in Benton, M.J. 1988b (*q.v.*).

Jerdon, T.C. 1874. *The mammals of India.* J. Wheldon, London; Thomson College Press, Roorkee.

Katti, M., Manjrekar, N., Mukherjee, S. & Sharma, D. 1990. A report on wildlife survey in Arunachal Pradesh with special reference to takin. Wildlife Institute of India, Dehra Dun.

Kelaart, E.F. 1850. Description of additional mammals. *J. Ceylon Br. R. Asiatic Soc.* 2: 216–217 (329–330 in reprint of 1890).

—— 1852, 1853. *Prodromus Faunae Zeylanicae* ... Published by author, 197, 66 pp. Colombo.

Kerr, R. 1792. *The animal kingdom ... Class I mammalia.* Murrey, London. 400pp. on official list of works approved as available for use in zoological nomenclature: Opinion 890 (1969).

Khajuria, H. 1953. Catalogue of mammals in the Zoological Survey of India, pt. 1, primates: hominoides. *Records Ind. Museum* 50: 129–145. Delhi.

—— 1954a. Notes on the systematics of three leaf monkeys in the collection of the Indian Museum (Zoological Survey). *Records Ind. Museum* (Delhi) 52: 95–99.

—— 1954b. Catalogue of mammals in the Indian Museum (Zoological Survey), pt. 2, primates: cercopithecidae. *Records Ind. Museum* (Delhi) 52: 101–127.

—— 1954c. Catalogue of mammals in the Indian Museum (Zoological Survey), pt. 3, primates: colobidae. *Records Ind. Museum* (Delhi) 52: 195–220.

—— 1955. Catalogue of mammals in the Zoological Survey of India, pt. 4, primates: prosimii, tarsioidii and platyrrhineae. *Records Ind. Museum* (Delhi) 53: 223–250.

—— 1956. A new langur ... From Goalpara district, Assam. *Annals. Mag. Nat. Hist.* 9: 86–88.

—— 1962. Further observations on Gee's langur, *Presbytis geei* Khajuria, with remarks on the classification of Indian colobidae (Mammalia: primates). *Records Ind. Museum* (Delhi) 58: 123–131.

Kloss, C.B. 1918. Notes on some hares in the Indian Museum ... *Records Indian Mus. Calcutta* 15: 89–96.

Koopman, K.F. 1982–1985. A synopsis of the families of bats. Parts I–VII, errata. *Bat Res. News* 23: 15–16, 26–27; 24: 1–2, 17–18, 36–38; 25: 15–17, 29; 26: 5.

—— 1984. Bats. pp. 145–186 in Anderson, S. & Jones, J.K. (q.v.).

—— 1989. Distributional patterns of Indo-Malayan bats ... *American Mus. Novit.* 2942: 19pp.

Kuhl, H. 1819. Die deutschen fledermause. *Annalen Wetterauisch.* Ges. 4: 11–49, 185–215, 2pls.

Lal, J.P. 1984. Taxonomic status of the Indian subspecies of the Kelaart's pipistrelle, *Pipistrellus ceylonicus* Kelaart ... *Bulletin Zool. Surv. India* 6: 159–161.

Lambert, A.B. 1804. Description of *Bos frontalis,* a new species from india. *Transactions Linn. Soc. Lond.* 7: 57–59, pl. 4 (and pp. 302–305).

Leach, W.E. 1821. The characters of three new genera of bats without foliaceous appendages to the nose (pp. 69–72); the characters of seven genera of bats with foliaceous appendages to the nose (pp. 73–82). *Transactions Linn. Society London* 13: 69–82.

Lekagul, B. & Mcneely, J.A. 1977. *Mammals of Thailand.* Assoc. Conservation Wildlife, Bangkok. Li, 758pp (reprinted in 1988).

Lindsay, H.M. 1929. Indian shrews. *J. Bombay Nat. Hist. Soc.* 33: 326–340.

Linnaeus, C. 1758. *Systema Naturae* ... Vol. 1, 10th ed. Holmia: 824pp.

—— 1766. *Systema Naturae,* 12th ed., 532pp.

Lu, H-G & Sheng, H-L. 1984. Status of the black muntjac, *Muntiacus crinifrons,* in eastern China. *Mammal Rev.* 14: 29–36.

Luckett, W.P. (ed.) 1980. *Comparative biology and evolutionary relationships of tree shrews.* Plenum Press, New York & London. XV, 314pp.

Luckett, W.P. & Hartenberger, J.L. 1985. *Evolutionary relationships among rodents* ... Plenum Press, New York & London . 721pp.

Lydekker, R. 1905. The gorals of India and Burma. *Zoologist* 9: 81–84.

—— 1907. The Bhutan takin. *Field* 110: 887.

—— 1924. *The game animals of India, Burma, Malaya and Tibet.* Rowland Ward, London.

Ma, S., Han, L. & Lan, D. 1994. *Bird and mammal resources and nature conservation in the Gaoligongshan Region, Yunan province, People's Republic of China.* Conservation Biology Center, Kunming Institute of Zoology, Kunming.

Ma, S., Wang, Y. & Liming, S. 1990. A new species of the genus *Muntiacus* from Yunnan, China. *Zoological Res.* 11: 47–53.

Mandal, A.K. 1984. A note on the distribution of the little Indian field mouse, *Mus booduga* ... *Bull. Zool. Survey India* 6: 301–303.

Marshall, J. 1976, 1977. Family Muridae (rats and mice). pp. 397–487 in Lekagul & Mc-neely, 1977 (*q.v.*). (distributed separately in 1976—see Musser, 1981: 237).

Martin, W. [C.L.] 1837. [A new species of the genus *Felis*.] *Proceedings Zool. Soc. Lond.* (1836): 107–108.

McCann, C. 1933a. Notes on the colouration and habits of the white-browed gibbon or hoolock (*Hylobates hoolock* Harl.). *J. Bombay Nat. Hist. Soc.* 36: 395–405.

—— 1933b. Observations on some of the Indian langurs. *J. Bombay Nat. Hist. Soc.* 36: 618–628.

—— 1933c. Notes on some Indian macaques . *J. Bombay Nat. Hist. Soc.* 36: 796–810.

Mcclelland, J. 1839. List of mammalia and birds collected in Assam. *Proceedings Zool. Soc. Lond.* 7: 146–167.

Mech, L.D. 1974. *Canis lupus. Mammalian Species* 37: 6pp.

Meyer, F.A.A. 1793. *Systematische-summarische uebersicht der neuersten zoologischen entdeckungen* ... Leipzig, 198pp.

—— 1794. Ueber de la metheries schwarzen panther. *Zoologische Annalen Weimer* 1: 394–396.

Miller, G.S. 1898. List of bats collected by Dr. W.L. Abbott in Siam. *Proceedings Acad. Nat. Sci. Philad.*: 316–325.

—— 1907. The families and genera of bats.*Bulletin US natn. Mus.* 57: XXVII, 282pp, 14pls.

Milne-Edwards, A. 1867a. Observations sur quelques mammifères du nord de la Chine. *Annales Sci. Nat., Zool.* (5)7: 375–377; 8: 374–376.

—— 1867b. Description de quelques especes nouvelles d'ecureuils ... *Revue Mag. Zool.* 19: 193–197; 225–232.

—— 1870. Note sur quelques mammifères du Thibet oriental. *Compte R. Acad. Sci. Paris* 70: 341–342.

—— 1872a. [Description of mammals— footnotes] pp. 91–93 in David, A., Rapport adresse a mm les professeurs administrateurs du museum d'histoire naturelle. *Nouvelles Archs Mus. Hist. Nat. Paris* 7: 73–100.

—— 1872b. 1874. Memoire sur la faune mammalogique du Tibet oriental. pp. 231–304 (1872), 305–386 (1874) in *Recherches Pour Servir a l'histoire des mammiferes.* Masson, Paris

Milroy, A.J.W. 1935. The preservation of wild life in India, nr. 3. Assam. *J. Bombay Nat. Hist. Soc.* 37 (1, suppl.): 97–104.

Mitchell, R.M. 1978. The *Ochotona* (Lagomorpha: Ochotonidae) of Nepal. *Säugetierkundliche Mitteilungen*, 26: 208–214.

Moore, J.C. & Tate, G. H. H. 1965. A study of the diurnal squirrels, sqiurinae, of the Indian and Indo-Chinese Subregions. *Fieldiana Zool.* 48: 1–351.

Mukherjee, R.P. 1978. Further observations on the golden langur (*Presbytis geei* Khajuria), with note on capped langur (*P. pileatus* Blyth) of Assam, India. *Proceedings wild life workshop*, Zool. Surv. Ind., pp. 129–132.

—— 1974. Phayre's leaf monkey (*P. phayrei* Blyth) of Tripura. *J. Bombay Nat. Hist. Soc.* 79: 47–56.

Müller, S. 1776... ... ... *Natursyst. Suppl. Regist. Band*, 40.

—— 1838. Over eenige nieuwe zoogdieren van Borneo. *Tijdschrift Natuurl. Gesch. Physiol.* 5: 134–150.

Musser, G.G. 1981. Notes on the systematics of Indo-Malayan murid rodents ... *Bull.American Mus. Nat. Hist.* 168: 225–334.

Musser, G.G. & Carleton, M.D. 1993. Family Muridae. pp. 501–756 in Wilson, D.E. & Reeder, D. M. (*q.v.*).

Musser, G.G. & Heaney, L.R. 1985. Phillippine *Rattus*: a new species from the Sulu Archipelago. *American Mus. Novit.* 2818: 32pp.

Musser, G.G. & Newcomb, C. 1983. Malaysian murids and the giant rat of Sumatra. *Bulletin Am. Mus. Nat. Hist.* 174: 329–598.

Myers, N. 1988. Threatened biotas:"hotspots" in tropical forests. *Environmentalist* 8 (3): 1–20.

—— 1991. The biodiversity challenge: expanded "hotspots" analysis. *Environmentalist* 10 (4): 243–256.

Oboussier, H. & Maydell, G.A. Von. 1959. Zur kenntnis des indischen goldlangurs, ergebnisee der deutschen indien-expedition 1955–57, Leitung G. A. Frhr. V. Maydell. *Zeitschrift fur morphologie und okologie der tiere* (Berlin), Vol. 48: 102–114.

Ogilby, W. 1837. [Generic distinction among the Ruminantia.] *Proceedings Zool. Soc. Lond.* (1836): 131–139.

—— 1839. Royle's ill. *Botany Himalaya*, LXIX, pl. 4.

Ognev, S.I. 1931. *Mammals of eastern Europe and northern Asia, Vol.* 2. Moscow (English translation Jerusalem, 1962).

Ohtaishi, N. & Gao, Y. 1990. A review of the distribution of all species of deer ... in China. *Mammal Rev.* 20: 125–144.

Oliver, W.L.R.1980. The pigmy hog: the biology & conservation of the pigmy hog and the hispid hare. *Special Scientific Report* no.1. The Jersey Wildlife Preservation Trust, Jersey.

Osgood, W.H. 1932. Mammals of the Kelley-Roosevelts and Delacour Asiatic expeditions. *Publications Field Mus. Nat. Hist. Zool.* 18: 193–339.

Pallas, P.S. 1766. *Miscellanea zoologica* ... Hagae comitum, 224pp.
—— 1767. *Spicilegia zoologica ... animalium species.* Berlin.
—— 1771, 1773. *Reise durch verschiedene provinzen des russischen reichs.* St. Petersberg.
—— 1778, 1779. *Novae species quadrupedum e glirum ordine* ... Walther, Erlangae.pp. 1–69 (1778), 70–388 (1779).
—— 1811. *Zoographia Rosso-Asiatica* ... Vol. 1. Petropoli, 568pp.
Parsons, R.E. 1941. Rivers as barriers to the distribution of gibbons. *J. Bombay Nat. Hist. Soc.* 42: 434 & 926.
Peters, W. 1872. Mitteilung uber neue flederthiere... *Monatsberichte k . Preuss Akad. Wiss.*: 256–264.
Peterson, R.L. 1968. Notes on an unusual specimen of *Scotophilus* from Vietnam. *Canadian J. Zool.* 46: 1079–1081.
Pocock, R.I. 1908. Notes upon some species and geographical races of serows (*Capricornis*) ... *Abstracts Proc. Zool. Soc. Lond.*: 12; *proc. Zool. Soc. Lond.*: 173–202.
—— 1914. Description of a new species of goral ... *J. Bombay Nat. Hist. Soc.* 23: 32–33.
—— 1931. The pig-tailed macaques (*Macaca nemestrina*). *J. Bombay Nat. Hist. Soc.* 35: 297–311.
—— 1933a. The civet cats of Asia. *J. Bombay Nat. Hist. Soc.* 36: 423–449; 629–656.
—— 1933b. The rarer genera of oriental viverridae. *Proceedings Zool. Soc. Lond.*: 969–1035, pls 1–3.
—— 1934. The palm civets or 'toddy cats' ... *J. Bombay Nat. Hist. Soc.* 37: 172–192; 314–346.
—— 1939, 1941. *The fauna of British India: mammalia. Primates and carnivora.* Taylor & Francis, London.
—— 1940. The hog-badgers (*Arctonyx*) of British India. *J. Bombay Nat. Hist. Soc.* 41: 461–469.
Prater, S.H. 1948. *The book of Indian animals.* Bombay Natural History Society, Bombay (now in its 4th edn.).
Prothero, D.R. & Schoch, R.M. (eds.) 1989. *The evolution of Perissodactyls.* Oxford UP, 320pp.

Rabinowitz, A. & Saw Tun Khaing. 1998. Status of selected mammal species in north Myanmar. *Oryx* 32 (3): 201–208.
Rabinowitz, A., Amato, G. & Saw Tun Khaing. 1998. Discovery of the black muntjac *Muntiacus crinifrons,* in north Myanmar. *Mammalia* 62 (1).
Raffles, T.S. 1821. Descriptive catalogue of a zoological collection made ... in Sumatra. *Transactions Linn. Soc. Lond.* 13: 239–340.

Rafinesque, C.S. 1814. *Precis de decourtes et travaux somiologiques ...* Palerme, 55pp.

—— 1832. description of a new otter, *Lutra concolor* from Assam in India. *Atlantic j.* 1: 62.

Reeves, R.R. & Brownell, R.L. 1989. Susu *Platanista gangetica ... Platanista minor* ... pp. 69–100 in Ridgeway, S.H. & Harrison, R. (*q.v.*).

Roberts, M.S. & Gittelman, J.L. 1984. *Ailurus fulgens. Mammalian Species* 222: 8pp.

Robinson, H.C. & Kloss, C.B. 1914. On new mammals ... from the Malay peninsula. *Annals. Mag. Nat. Hist.* 13: 223–234.

—— 1919. On a collection of mammals from ... Sumatra. *J. Fed. Malay States Mus.* 7: 257–291.

—— 1922. New mammals from french Indo-China and Siam. *Annals Mag. Nat. Hist.* 9: 87–99.

Rookmaaker, L.C. 1980.the distribution of the rhinoceros in eastern India, Bangladesh, China, and the Indo-Chinese Region. *Zool. Anz., Jena* 205: 253–268.

Roonwal, M.L. & Mohnot, S.M. 1977. *Primates of South Asia: ecology, sociobiology & behaviour.* Harv. Univ. Press, Cambridge (Mass.).

Roxburgh, W. 1801. An account of a new species of *Delphinus ... Asiatick Researches* [Calcutta ed.] 7: 170–174.

Ryley, K.V. 1914. Scientific results from the mammal survey VI. *J. Bombay Nat. Hist. Soc.* 22: 658–664.

Saha, S.S. 1977. A new subspecies of the flying squirrel, *Petaurista nobilis* (Gray), from Bhutan. *Proc. Zool. Soc., Calcutta* 28 (1975): 27–29.

—— 1981. A new genus and a new species of flying squirrel ... from northern India. *Bulletin Zool. Surv. India* 4: 331–336.

—— 1984. Occurrence of the tail-less fruit bat *Megaerops ecaudatus* ... in Arunachal Pradesh ... *Bulletin Zool. Surv. India* 6: 343–344.

—— 1985. Mammalia. *Rec. Zool. Surv. India* 82 (1–4): 321–330.

Saharia, V.B. 1982. *Wildlife in India.* Natraj Pub., Dehra Dun.

Sankhala, K. 1978. *Tiger ! The story of the Indian tiger.* Collins, London.

Savi, P. 1822. *Nuovo giorn. Lett. Sci. Pisa* 1: 60 (*n. v.*).

Schaller, G.B. 1977. *Mountain monarchs. Wild sheep and goats of the Himalaya.* Chicago University Press, Chicago.

—— 1973. On the behaviour of blue sheep (*Pseudois nayaur*). *J. Bombay Nat. Hist. Soc.* 69: 523–537.

Schlitter, D.A. & Thonglongya, K. 1971. *Rattus turkestanicus* ... the valid name for *Rattus rattoides* ... Proc. Biol. Soc. Washington 84: 171–174.

Schreber, J.C.D. von 1774–1785. *Die saugethiere in abbildungen nach der natur* ... Erlangen: 1112pp, 347pls.

Sclater, P.L. 1875. [Exhibition of, and remarks on, the upper horn of a two-horned rhino-ceros from the valley of the Brahmapootra.] *Proc. Zool. Soc. Lond.*: 566.

—— 1885. [Report on the additions to the society's menagerie ...] *Proc. Zool. Soc. Lond.*: 1–2, pl. 1.

Scully, J. 1881. On the mammals of Gilgit. *Proceedings Zool. Soc. Lond.*: 197–209.

Seba, A. 1734. *Locupletissimi rerum naturalium* ... Amsterdam.

Seshadri, B. 1969. *The twilight of India's wild life*. John Baker, London.

Severtzov, N. 1858. Notice sur la classification multiseriale des carnivores ... *Revue Mag. Zool.* 10: 385–393.

Shaw, G. 1800, 1801. *General zoology ... Vol. I, Vol. II, part i. Mammalia*. London: 553, 226pp.

Shaw, G. & Nodder, F.P. 1791. *The naturalist's miscellany* Vol. 2. Nodder, London.

Shebbeare, E. O. 1953. Status of the three Asiatic rhinoceros. *Oryx* 2: 141–149.

Singh, G. 1976. *A geography of india*. Atma Ram & Sons, Delhi.

Singh, P. 1991. A preliminary faunal survey in Thingbu Circle, Towang district, Arunachal Pradesh. *Arunachal Forest News* 9 (1): 13–22.

Singh, P., Haridasan, K., Borang, A., Bhatt, B., Borooah, C. & Borah, M. 1994. baseline survey of biodiversity in high priority biologically rich areas of Arunachal Pradesh–Tale Valley. Interim report to WWF-India, Itanagar.

Singh, P., Haridasan, K., Borang, A., Bhatt, B., Borooah, C., Borah, M. & Limbu, D. 1995. Baseline survey of biodiversity in high priority biologically rich areas of Arunachal Pradesh–Dichu Valley. Interim report to WWF-India, Itanagar.

Singh, P., Haridasan, K., Borang, A., Bhatt, B., Limbu, D. & Borah, M. 1996. Baseline survey of biodiversity in high priority biologically rich areas of Arunachal Pradesh–Mouling area. Interim report to WWF-India, Itanagar.

Smith, C.H. 1827. The carnassiers (Vol. 2); Order VII—Ruminantia (Pecora, Lin.). (Vol. 4: 1–428; Vol. 5: 296–376) in Griffith, E. *et al., Cuvier's animal kingdom . Synopsis of the species of the class mammalia*. Whittaker, London.

Sody, H.J.V. 1946. Review of: prehistoric and fossil rhinoceroses of the Malay archipelago and India, by D.A. Hooijer. *Natuurwetenschappelijk tijdschr. Ned. Indie* 102: 151.

—— 1959. Das javanische nashorn *Rhinoceros sondaicus. Zeitschrift saugetierk.* 24: 109–240.

Sparrman, A. 1778. Beskrifning pa *Sciurus bicolor,* et nytt species ikorn, fran Java. *Handlingar gotheb. Wet. Saml. Wet. Afd.* 1: 70–71.

Sterndale, R.A. 1884. *Natural history of Indian mammals.* Thacker, Spink, Calcutta.

Stoliczka, F. 1872. Notice of the mammals and birds inhabiting Kachh. *J. Asiatic Soc. Bengal* 41, 2: 211–258.

Stracey, P.D. 1963a. *Elephant gold.* Weidenfeld & Nicholson.

—— 1963b. *Wild life in India: its conservation & control.* Ministry of Food & Agriculture, Department of Agriculture, government of India, New Delhi.

Sukumar, R. 1989. *The Asian elephant: ecology and management.* Cambridge Univ. Press, Cambridge. 251pp.

Swinhoe, R. 1871. Catalogue of the mammals of China ... *Proceedings Zool. Soc. Lond.* (1870): 615–653.

Tate, G.H.H. 1941. Notes on vespertilionid bats. *Bulletin Am. Mus. Nat. Hist.* 78: 567–597.

—— 1942. Review of the vespertilionine bats ... *Bulletin Am. Mus. Nat. Hist.* 80: 221–297.

—— 1947. *Mammals of eastern Asia.* Macmillan, New York.

Temminck, C.J. 1834. Over een geslachk der vleugelhandige zoogdieren ... *Tijdschrift Natuurl. Gesch. Physiol.* 1: 1–30, 1pl.

—— 1835, 1837, 1840, 1841. *Monographies de mammalogie* ... Tome 2. Leiden & Paris. 392pp, pls XXVI–LXX.

—— [1836]. *Coup d'oeil sur la faune des iles de la sonde et de l'empire du japon.* Leiden, 30pp.

—— 1838. Over de geslachten *Taphozous, Emballonura, urocryptus en diclidurus. tijdschrift natuurl. Gesch. Physiol.* 5: 3–34, 1pl.

Templeton, W.E. 1848. In Blyth, E., Report of curator ... *J. Asiatic Soc. Bengal* 17: 247–255.

Thomas, O. 1882. Description of a new species of rat from China. *Proceedings Zool. Soc.Lond.*: 587–588, pl. 44.

—— 1886a. Diagnoses of three new oriental mammals. *Annals Mag. Nat. Hist.* 17: 84.

—— 1886b. On the mammals presented by Allan O. Hume ... *Proceedings Zool. Soc. Lond.*: 54–79, pls 5,6.

Thomas, O. 1888. *Eupetaurus,* a new form of flying squirrel from Kashmir. *J. Asiatic Soc. Bengal* 57,2: 256–260.

—— 1891. Diagnoses of three new mammals ... in Burma. *Annali Mus. Civ. Stor. Nat. Giacomo Doria* 10: 884.

—— 1908. On the generic position of groups of squirrels typified by "*Sciurus*" *berdmorei* and *pernyi* ... *J. Bombay Nat. Hist. Soc.* 18: 244–249.

—— 1911a. [Mammals collected in ... W. China ...] *Abstracts Proc. Zool. Soc. Lond.* 90: 3–5.

—— 1911b. The Duke of Bedford's exploration of E. Asia. XIII. On mammals from the provinces of Kan-su and Sze-chwan, W. China. *Proc. Zool. Soc. Lond.*: 158–180.

—— 1911c. [Mammals in ... W. China ...] *Abstracts Proc. Zool. Soc. Lond.* 100: 48–50.

—— 1912. The Duke of Bedford's zoological exploration of eastern Asia. XV. On mammals from the provinces of Szechuan and Yunnan, western China. *Proceedings Zool. Soc. Lond.*: 127–141.

—— 1914a. A new *Soriculus* from the Mishmi hills. *J. Bombay Nat. Hist. Soc.* 22: 683.

—— 1914b. On small mammals collected in Tibet and the Mishmi hills ... *J. Bombay Nat. Hist. Soc.* 23: 230–233.

—— 1915a. On bats of the genera *Nyctalus, Tylonycteris,* and *Pipistrellus. Annals. Mag. Nat. Hist.* 15: 225–232.

—— 1915b. On pipistrelles of the genera *Pipistrellus* and *Scotozous. J. Bombay Nat. Hist. Soc.* 24: 29–36.

—— 1915c. Scientific results from the mammal survey, X. *J. Bombay Nat. Hist. Soc.* 23: 607–613a.

—— 1916a. Scientific results from the mammal survey, XIII. *J. Bombay Nat. Hist. Soc.* 24: 404–430.

—— 1916b. A new rat from Tenasserim. *Annals Mag. Nat. Hist.* 17: 425.

—— 1917. Scientific results from the mammal survey, XVI. *J. Bombay Nat. Hist. Soc.* 25: 199–206.

—— 1921a. Scientific results from the mammal survey, XXV. *J. Bombay Nat. Hist. Soc.* 27: 596–599.

—— 1921b. Two new rats from Assam. *J. Bombay Nat. Hist. Soc.* 28: 26–27.

—— 1921c. The geographical races of *Scotomanes ornatus. J. Bombay Nat. Hist. Soc.* 27: 772–773.

—— 1922a. On mammals from the Yunnan highlands ... *Annals. Mag . Nat. Hist.* 10: 391–406.

—— 1922b. Scientific results of the mammal survey, XXXII. *J. Bombay Nat. Hist. Soc.* 28: 428–432.

Thomas, O. 1923. On mammals from Li-kiang Range, Yunnan ... *Annals. Mag . Nat. Hist.* 9,11: 662.

—— 1929. The delacour exploration of French Indo-China—mammals. LII ... *Proceedings Zool. Soc. Lond.* (1928): 831–841.

Thomas, O. & Wroughton, R.C. 1916. On the squirrels obtained ... on the Chindwin river, upper Burma ... *J. Bombay Nat. Hist. Soc.* 24: 224–239.

Tikader, B.K. 1983. *Threatened animals of India*. Zoological Survey of India, Calcutta.

Tilson, R.L. 1979. Behaviour of hoolock gibbons (*H. hoolock*) during different seasons in Assam. *J. Bombay nat. Hist. Soc.* 76: 1–16.

Tomes, R.F. 1856. Pp. 22–23 in Blyth, E., Memoir on the Indian species of shrews. *Annals Mag. Nat. Hist.* 17: 11–28.

Topal, G. 1970. On the systematic status of *Pipistrellus annectans* ... *Annales Hist.-Nat. Mus. Natn. Hung. Zool.* 62: 373–379.

Tytler, R.C. 1854. Miscellaneous notes on the fauna of Dacca ... *Annals. Mag. Nat. Hist.* 14: 168–177.

Vahl, M. 1797. Beskrivelse paa tre nye arter flagermuse. *Skrifter naturh.-selsk. kiobenhavn* 4: 121–138.

Vanak, A.T.F. & Goyal, S.P. 1996. Survey of fruit bats in Namdapha tiger reserve. Wildlife Institute of India, Dehra Dun.

Van valen, L. 1967. New palaeocene insectivores and insectivore classification. *Bulletin Am. Mus. Nat. Hist.* 135: 219–284.

—— 1979. The evolution of bats. *Evolution Theory* 4: 103–121.

Van weers, D.J. 1979. Notes on southeast Asian porcupines ... 4. On the taxonomy of the subgenus *Acanthion* ... *Beaufortia* 29: 215–272.

Vigors, A.A. & Horsfield, T. 1827. Description of two species of the genus *Felis*. *Zoological J.* 3: 449–451, pl. 12.

—— 1828. Observations ... mammalia ... Museum of the Zool. Soc. *Zool. J.* 4: 105–113.

Wagner, J.A. 1839. Beschreibung einiger neuer oder wenig bekannter saugethiere. *Gelehrte anz. Akad. Wiss. Munchen* 9(184): 433–440.

—— 1841. *Die saugethiere in abbildungen nach der natur* ... Suppl. 2, Raubthiere. Weigel., Leipzig.

Wang, Y., Luo, Z. & Feng, Z. 1985. Taxonomic revision of Yunnan hare, *Lepus comus* ... *Zoological Res.* 6: 101–109.

Waterhouse, G.R. 1843. [Proceedings of Zoological Society meeting, October 11, 1842.] *Annals Mag. Nat. Hist.* 12: 130–135.

Wayre, P. 1968. Some observations on the golden langur *P. Geei* (MS Khajuria) Gee. *J. Bombay Nat. Hist. Soc.* 65: 473–477.

West, E. 1926. Takin shooting in the spring. *J. Bombay Nat. Hist. Soc.* 31: 273–275.

Weston, M.L. 1982. A numerical revision of the genus Ochotona (Lagomorpha: Mammalia) and an examination of its phylogenetic relationships. Unpub. Ph.D. dissertation, Univ. of British Columbia, Vancouver, 387 pp.

Wilson, A. 1924. *Sport and service in Assam and elsewhere.* 256 Hutchinson & Co., London.

Wilson, D.E. & Reeder, D.M. (eds.). 1993. *Mammal species of the world: a taxonomic & geographic reference.* 2nd edn. Smithsonian Institution Press, Washington, D.C. & London.

Wirth, R. & Groves, C.P. 1988. A new deer in China. *Species* 11: 15.

Wood, H.S. 1930. Observations on Indian rhino and their shikar on foot. *J. Darjeeling Nat. Hist. Soc.* 4: 59–69.

Wozencraft, W..C. 1989a. The phylogeny of the recent carnivora. pp. 495–535 in Gittelman, J.L., (*q.v.*).

—— 1989b. Appendix: classification of the recent carnivora. pp. 560–593 in Gittelman, J.L., (*q.v.*).

Wroughton, R.C . 1899. Some Konkan bats. *J. Bombay Nat. Hist. Soc.* 12: 716–725.

—— 1915. The Burmese civets. *J. Bombay Nat. Hist. Soc.* 24: 63–64.

—— 1916a. Bombay Natural History Society's mammal survey ... Report no. 26. Darjiling district. *J. Bombay Nat. Hist. Soc.* 24: 773–782.

—— 1916b. The langurs of Assam. *J. Bombay Nat. Hist. Soc.* 24: 653–655.

—— 1916c. New rodents from Sikkim. *J. Bombay Nat. Hist. Soc.* 24: 425–430.

—— 1918. Summary of the results from the Indian mammal survey. Parts 1 & 2. *J. Bombay Nat. Hist. Soc.* 25: 547–598; 26: 19–58.

—— 1921a. Scientific results from the mammal survey, XXVI. *J. Bombay Nat. Hist. Soc.* 27: 599–601.

—— 1921b. On the *Erythraeus* group of squirrels. *J. Bombay Nat. Hist. Soc.* 27: 773–777.

Yenbutra, S. & Felten, H. 1983. A new species of the fruit bat genus *Megaerops* from S.E. Asia ... *Senckenbergiana Biol.* 64: 1–11.

Zimmermann, E.A.W. 1777. *Specimen zoologiae geographicae, quadrupedum* ... Lugduni Batavorum: XXIV, 685pp.

—— 1780. *Geographische geschichte des menschen* ... Leipzig.

[illegible] of [illegible]

[illegible]

[illegible] [illegible] from [illegible]

INDEX

A

abramus, Pipistrellus, 26
adustus, Cuon a., 43, 44
affinis, Cervus, 70
affinis, Felis, 57
affinis, Pipistrellus, 28
affinis, Rhinolophus, 22
Ailuridae, 47
albifrons, Paradoxurus, 55
albiventer, Pteromys, 85
alboniger, Hylopetes, *Sciuropterus,* 87
alborufus, Pteromys, 85
alpinus, Cuon, *Canis,* 43
ammon, Ovis, *Capra,* 79
andersoni, Niviventer, *Epimys,* 94
angulatus, Cynopterus, 18
annectans, Myotis, *Pipistrellus,* 25
anthonyi, Pipistrellus, 102
Anthropoidea, 31, 102
aquilo, Callosciurus castaneoventris, 82
arctoides, Macaca, *Macacus,* 37
arctos, Ursus, 44
Argali, 79
argali, Tibetan, 80
armiger, Hipposideros, *Rhinolophus,* 23
arnee, Bubalus, *Bos,* 74
Artiodactyla, 67, 102
Arvicolinae, 95, 102
assamensis, Atherurus, 97
assamensis, Macaca, 34, 35, 36, 37
attenuata, Crocidura, 13
aurata, Murina, 29
aureus, Canis, 42
auritus, Manis, 9
auropunctata, Mangusta, 55
austriacus, Plecatus, 101

B

babu, Pipistrellus, 27
badger, Eurasian, 49
badius, Cannomys, *Rhizomys,* 96
baileyi, Naemorhedus, 77
baileyi, Soriculus, 12
bamboo rat, Bay, or Lesser, 96
bamboo rat, Hoary, 95
bandicoot-rat, Lesser, 91
bandicoot-rat, Large, 90
baptistae, Viverricula i., 53
Barasingha, 69
barbastelle, Eastern, 25
bat, Asiatic greater yellow house, 26
bat, Asiatic lesser yellow house, 25
bat, Bamboo, 26
bat, Big-eared horseshoe, 21
bat, Black-bearded tomb, 20
bat, Blanford's or Mountain fruit, 19
bat, Blyth's horseshoe, 21
bat, Burmese whiskered, 101
bat, Chocolate, 28
bat, Club-footed bat, 26
bat, Daubenton's or Water, 25
bat, Dawn or Cave fruit, 19
bat, European free-tailed, 31
bats, Evening, 101
bats, False vampire, 20
bat, Flat-headed, 26
bats, Free-tailed, 31
bat, Fulvous fruit, 18
bat, Fulvous leaf-nosed, 23
bat, Greater false vampire, Indian false vampire, 21
bat, Greater horseshoe, 22
bat, Greater mouse-tailed, 101
bat, Greater tube-nosed, 29
bat, Great evening, 102
bat, Grey long-eared, 101
bat, Hairy-faced, 25
bat, Hairy-winged, 30
bat, Harlequin, 25
bat, Himalayan leaf-nosed, 23
bat, Himalayan whiskered, 24
bat, Hodgson's, 24
bats, Horseshoe, 101

bat, Hutton's tube-nosed, 29
bat, Intermediate horseshoe, 22
bat, Large leaf-nosed, 23
bat, Least horseshoe, 22
bat, Least leaf-nosed, 23
bat, Lesser dog-faced fruit, 18
bat, Lesser false vampire, 20
bat, Little tube-nosed, 29
bat, Long-tongued hill fruit, 19
bat, Long-winged tomb, 20
bat, Miller's fruit, 18
bats, Mouse-tailed, 101
bat, Naked-rumped tomb, 20
bat, Orange tube-nosed, 30
bats, Old world fruit, 16
bats, Old world leaf-nosed, 22, 101
bat, Painted, 30
bat, Pouch-bearing, 20
bat, Round-eared tube-nosed, 30
bat, Rufous horseshoe, 22
bat, Schreibers' long-fingered, 28
bats, Sheath-tailed, 20
bat, Short-nosed, 18
bat, Tail-less fruit, 19
bat, Tail-less leaf-nosed, 101
bat, Thick-eared, 26
bat, Thomas's horseshoe, 101
bat, Tickell's, 28
bat, Trefoil horseshoe, 21
bats, Trident, 22, 101
bats, Tube-nosed, 29
bat, Whiskered, 24
bat, Woolly horseshoe, 21
bat, Wrinkle-lipped free-tailed, 31
bear, Brown, 44
Bear-cat, 54
bear, Himalayan black, Asiatic black, 44
bear, Sloth, 46
bear, Sun, Malayan, 45
bear, Tibetan blue, 44
bedfordiae, Sorex, 11
belangeri, Tupaia, *Cladobates,* 15
Belomys, 84
bengalensis, Bandicota, *Arvicola,* 91
bengalensis, Elephas m., 65
bengalensis, Felis, 57
bengalensis, Vulpes, *Canis,* 43
berezovskii, Moschus, 69
Bharal, 78, 79, 80
bhotia, Rattus r., 89
bhutanensis, Sciurus e., 81
bicolor, Hipposideros, 23
bicolor, Ratufa, *Sciurus,* 80
binturong, Arctictis, *Viverra,* 54
'bison', Indian, 73
biswasi, Biswamoyopterus, 87
blanfordi, Sphaerias, *Cynopterus,* 19
blythii, Macaca nemestrina, 33
blythii, Sciurus, 82
boar, Wild, 67
bobak, Marmota, *Mus,* 84
booduga, Mus, *Leggada,* 88
bowersii, Berylmys, *Mus,* 94
brachyura, Hystrix, 96
brachyotis,Cynopterus, *Pachysoma,* 18
brachypterus, Philetor, 102
brahma, Niviventer, *Epimys,* 93
brahma, Presbytis, 38
brunneusculus, Mus, 89
bubalis, Bubalus, 74
buffalo, Wild water, Asiatic wild, 74

C

cadornae, Pipistrellus, 28
Callosciurinae, 81
candidulas, Pteromys, 85
caniceps, Petaurista, *Sciuropterus,* 85
Canidae, 42
Caprinae, 75
Carnivora, Carnivores, 41, 102
castaneus, Mus, 87
cat, Fishing, 58
cat, Golden, 58
cat, Jungle, 57
cat, Leopard, 57
cat, Marbled, 58
Catopuma, 58
cat, Pallas's, 102
cat, Toddy, 54
caudata, Antilope, 76
caudatus, Soriculus, *Sorex,* 12
cephalophus, Elaphodus, 102
Cercopithecidae, 33, 102
Cercopithecinae, 33
cervicolor, Mus, 88
Cervidae, 68, 102
Cervinae, 69, 102
Cetacea, 62
ceylonicus, Pipistrellus, *Scotophilus,* 26
chanco, Canis lupus, 42
charltonii, Felis m., 59
chaus, Felis, 57
Chiroptera, 16, 101
chrysogaster, Moschus, 69
cineraceus, Hipposideros, 23
cinerea, Aonyx, *Lutra,* 52

cinereus, Eupetaurus, 86
circumdatus, Pipistrellus, 102
civet, Common palm, 54
civet, Large Indian, 52
civet, Masked palm, Himalayan palm, 54
civet, Small Indian, 53
civet, Small-toothed palm, 55
collaris, Arctonyx, 50
Colobinae, 38, 102
concolor, Amblonyx, 52
confucianus, *Niviventer,* 102
consul, Arctonyx c., 50
cookii, Mus, 88
coromandra, Pipistrellus, *Scotophilus,* 27
coucang, Nycticebus, *Tardigradus,* 32
cranbrooki, Naemorhedus, 77
crassicaudata, Manis; 10, 101
cremoriventer, Rattus, 93
crinifrons, Muntiacus, *Cervulus,* 71
cristatus, Presbytis, 102
cristatus, Sus, 67
crumpi, Diomys, 102
curzoniae, Ochotona, 100
cyclotis, Murina, 30

D

darjelingensis, Plecotus, 25
daubentonii, Myotis, *Vespertilio,* 25
deer, Barking, 71
deer, Himalayan musk, 68
deer, Hog, 70
deer, Red, 70
deer, Swamp, 69
deer, Tibetan red, 70
deer, Tufted, 102
Dhole, 43
Didermocerus, 66
dog, Indian wild, Red, 43
dolphin, Gangetic, 63
draco, Apodemus, *Mus sylvaticus,* 91
dumeticola, Mus, 89
durga, Presbytis, 39
duvauceli, Cervus, 69

E

ecaudatus, Megaerops, 19
edwardsii, Herpestes, *Ichneumon,* 56
edwardsi, Leopoldamys, *Mus,* 94
eha, Niviventer, *Epimys,* 93
elaphus, Cervus, 70
elegans, Nectogale, 15
elegans, Petaurista, *Pteromys,* 85
elephant, Asian, Indian, 64
Elephantidae, 64
Elephas, 64
ellioti, Golunda, 90
Emballonuridae, 20
entellus, Semnopithecus, 38, 40
erythraeus, Callosciurus, *Sciurus,* 81, 82
erythrotis, Mus, 91
etruscus, Suncus, *Sorex,* 13
evansi, Urotragus, 76

F

famulus, Mus, 88
Felidae, 57, 102
ferret-badger, Burmese or Large-toothed, 50
ferret-badger, Chinese or Small-toothed, 51
ferrumequinum, Rhinolophus, 22
flavigula, Martes, *Mustela,* 49
flying fox, Indian, 17
flying squirrel, Common giant, or Red, 85
flying squirrel, Complex-toothed, 102
flying squirrel, Grey-headed giant, or Lesser giant, 85
flying squirrel, Hairy-footed, 84
flying squirrel, Hodgson's, 86
flying squirrel, Lesser giant, 85
flying squirrel, Namdapha, 87
flying squirrel, Particoloured, 87
flying squirrel, Temminck's, 102
flying squirrel, Woolly, 86
foina, Martes, *Mustela,* 48
formosus, Myotis, 24
forresti, Ochotona, 99
fox, Bengal, 43
fox, Red or Himalayan, 43
frithii, Coelops, 101
frontalis, Bos, 73
fulgens, Ailurus, 47
fulvescens, Niviventer, *Mus,* 93
fulvidina, Felis c., 57
fulvidus, Scotophilus, 26
fulvocinerea, Crocidura (Pachyura), 13
fulvus, Bubalus b., 74
fulvus, Hipposideros, 23
fusca, Felis, 60
fuscus, Moschus, 69
fusicauda, Scaptonyx, 101

G

gangetica, Platanista, 63
gangeticus, Delphinus, 63
garonum, Dremomys, 83
garonum, Rattus listeri, 94
Gaur, 73
gaurus, Bos, 73, 74
Gayal, 73
geei, Presbytis, 102
giant squirrel, Malayan, or Black giant, 80
gibbon, Hoolock or White-browed, 40
gigantea, Vespertilio, 17
giganteus, Pteropus, 17
giganteus, Sciurus, 81
gliroides, Chiropodomys, *Mus,* 91
glis, Tupaia, 16
gloveri, Ochotona, 102
gobiensis, Eptesicus, 101
golok, Simia, 40
gongshanensis, Muntiacus, 71
Goral, 76, 78
goral, Chinese, 76
goral, Himalayan, 76
goral, Naemorhedus, *Antilope,* 76
goral, Red, 77
gordoni, Callosciurus, 82
gordoni, Sciurus, 81
gracilis, Uropsilus, 101
griffithi, Sorex, 13
griseus, Naemorhedus, 76
gueldenstaedtii, Crocidura, *Sorex,* 14

H

hare, Hispid, 98
hare, Indian,or Rufous-tailed, 97
harpia, Harpiocephalus, *Vespertilio,* 30
heathii, Scotophilus, 26
Helarctos, 45
hermaphrodita, Viverra, 54
hermaphroditus, Paradoxurus, 54
Herpestidae, 55
himalayana, Marmota b., 84
himalayana, Ochotona, 100
himalayanus, Arctomys, 84
himalayica, Chimarrogale, 14
himalayicus, Crossopus, 14
Hipposideridae, 22, 101
hispidus, Caprolagus, *Lepus,* 98
hodgsoni, Acanthion, 96
hodgsoni, Naemorhedus, 76
hodgsonii, Ovis, 80
Hog-badger, 50
hog, Pygmy, Pigmy, 67
homourus, Mus, 87
hoolock, Hylobates, *Simia,* 40
horsfieldi, Crocidura, *Sorex,* 14
horsfieldii, Felis, 57
howelli, Dremomys p., 83
huttonii, Murina, *Harpiocephalus,* 29
Hylobatidae, 40
Hylobatinae, 40
Hystricidae, 96

I

indica, Bandicota, 90
indica, Hystrix, 97
indica, Viverricula, *Viverra,* 53
indicus, Canis aureus, 43
indicus, Mus, 90
Insectivora, 10, 101
intermedia, Sciurus, 81
io, Ia, 102

J

jackal, Golden, or Golden-backed, 42
jacksoniae, Leggada, 89
jamrachi, Capricornis, 77, 78
javanicus, Herpestes, *Ichneumon,* 55
javanicus, Pipistrellus, *Scotophilus,* 26, 27
jemlahicus, Hemitragus, 102
jerdoni, Rattus, 93
joffrei, Pipistrellus, 102
johnii, Presbytis, 38

K

kachhensis, Taphozous, 20
kathiah, M. (Putorices), 48
kathiah, Mustela, 48
Kerivoulinae, 30
kozlovi, Martes f. 48
kuhlii, Scotophilus, 25

L

labiata, Vespertilio, 28
Lagomorpha, 97
langbianis, Niviventer, *Rattus cremoriventer,* 93

langur, Capped, 38, 39
langur, Golden, 102
langur, Hanuman, or Gray, 40
lankadiva, Hipposideros, 23
larvata, Paguma, 54
larvatus, Gulo, 54
larvatus, Hipposideros, *Rhinolophus,* 23
lasiotis, Rhinoceros, 66
lasyura, Noctulinia, 30
latronum, Apodemus, 92
leaf monkey, Golden, 102
leoninus, Macaca, 33
Leopard, 60
leopard, Clouded, 59
leopard, Snow, 62
lepcha, Tupaia b., 16
lepidus, Rhinolophus, 21
Leporidae, 97
leptophylla, Phyllorhina, 23
leschenaulti, Rousettus, *Pteropus,* 18
leucogaster, Murina, 29
leucomelas, Barbastella, *Vespertilio,* 25
leucops, Soriculus, 12
leucura, Talpa, 11
leucurus, Meles m., 49
libonotus, Eothenomys m., 95
linsang, Spotted, 53
lokriah, Dremomys, *Sciurus,* 83
lokroides, Sciurus, 82
longimanus, Taphozous, 20
Loridae, Lorisidae, 32
loris, Slow, 32
Loxodonta, 63
luctus, Rhinolophus, 21
lupus, Canis, 42
lutra, Lutra, *Mustela,* 51
Lutrinae, 51
lynx, European, 102
lynx, Felis, 102
lyra, Megaderma, 21

M

macaque, Assamese, 34, 36
macaque, Père David's, 35, 36
macaque, Pig-tailed, 34, 36
macaque, Rhesus, 36
macaque, Stump-tailed, 37
macaque, Tibetan, 35
mackenziei, Berylmys, *Epimys,* 94
macmillani, Dremomys, 83
Macroglossinae, 19
macroselloides, Felis, 60
macrotis, Rhinolophus, 21
macrourus, Atherurus, *Hystrix,* 97
macrurus, Soriculus, 12
magnificus, Petaurista, *Sciuropterus,* 86
malayanus, Ursus, 45
Manidae, 9, 101
manipulus, Berylmys, *Epimys,* 94
manul, Felis, 102
marmorata, Felis, 58
marmot, Himalayan, 84
Marmotinae, 84
marten, Beech, or Stone, 48
marten, Yellow-throated, 49
maximus, Elephas, 64
mcclellandii, Tamiops, *Sciurus,* 82
Megachiroptera, 17
Megadermatidae, 20
melanogaster, Eothenomys, *Arvicola,* 95
melanopogon, Taphozous, 20
meles, Meles, *Ursus,* 49
Melinae, 49
Melursus, 46
Microchiroptera, 20, 101
microphyllum, Rhinopoma, 101
Microtinae, 95, 102
micrura, Talpa, 10
millardi, Dacnomys, 92
millsi, Arctogalidia, 55
millsi, Helictis, 51
minimus, M., 19
Miniopterinae, 28
minor, Rhinolophus, 22
minutus, Micromys, *Mus,* 91
Mithun, 73
mole, Himalayan or Indian short-tailed, 10
mole, Long-tailed, 101
mole-shrew, 14
mole, White-tailed, 11
Molossidae, 31
mongoose, Crab-eating, 56
mongoose, Indian grey, 56
mongoose, Small Asian, or Small Indian, 55
monkey, Rhesus, 36
monkey, Silvered leaf, 102
monticolus, Lutra, 52
montivagus, Myotis, 101
moschata, Melogale, *Helictis,* 51
moschiferus, Moschus, 68
Moschinae, 68
mouse, Crump's, 102
mouse, Fawn-coloured, 88

mouse-hare, Himalayan, 100
mouse, Harvest, 91
mouse, House, 87
mouse, Little Indian field, 88
mouse, Palm, Indian long-tailed tree, 89
mouse, Pencil-tailed tree, 91
mouse, Sikkim, 88
mouse, Wood, or Common field, 91
mulatta, Macaca, *Cercopithecus*, 36
muntjak, Black, 71
muntjak, Gongshan, 72
muntjak, Indian, 71
muntjak, Leaf, 72
muntjak, Muntiacus, *Cervus*, 71
muricola, Myotis, 24
Muridae, 87, 102
Murinae, 87, 102
Murininae, 29
murinus, Suncus, *Sorex*, 12
musculus, Mus, 87
Mustelidae, 48
Mustelinae, 48
mystacinus, Myotis, *Vespertilio*, 24

N

nagarum, Callosciurus e., 82
nagarum, Leggada, 88
Nayan, 78, 79
nayaur, Pseudois, *Ovis*, 79
nebulosa, Neofelis, *Felis*, 59
neglecta, Paguma l., 54
nemestrina, Macaca, *Simia*, 6, 33, 37
nemorivagus, Mus (Rattus), 90
nigrescens, Soriculus, *Corsira*, 11
nigricollis, Lepus, 97
nipalensis, Gulo, 50
niphanae, Megaerops, 19
nitidus, Rattus, *Mus*, 89
niviventer, Niviventer, *Mus (Rattus)*, 92
nobilis, Petaurista, *Sciuropterus*, 86
noctula, Nyctalus, *Vespertilio*, 28
noctule, Common, 28
nudipes, Sorex, 13
nudiventris, Taphozous, 20
nyula, Herpestes e., 56

O

Odontoceti, 63
obscurus, Presbytis, 38
Ochotonidae, 99
oleracea, Vandeleuria, 89
oleraceus, Mus, 89
orestes, Apodemus, 92
ornatus, Scotomanes, 25
otter, Common, or Eurasian, 51
otter, Oriental small-clawed, or Clawless, 52
otter, Smooth Indian, or Smooth-coated, 52
Ounce, 62

P

pachyotis, Eptesicus, *Vesperugo (Vesperus)*, 26
pachypus, Tylonycteris, *Vespertilio*, 26
pahari, Mus, 88
pallasii, Paradoxurus, 54
panda, Lesser, or Red, 47
pangolin, Indian, 10, 101
pangolin, Chinese, 9
Panther, 60
Paradoxurinae, 54
parca, Soriculus, 101
pardicolor, Prionodon, 53
Pardofelis, 59
pardus, Panthera, *Felis*, 60
paterculus, Pipistrellus, 26
pearsonii, Trogopterus, *Sciuropterus*, 84
pelops, Macaca, a., 34, 35
pentadactyla, Manis, 9
Perissodactyla, 65
pernyi, Dremomys, *Sciurus*, 83
personata, Melogale, 50
perspicillata, Lutrogale, *Lutra*, 52
petaurista, Petaurista, *Sciurus*, 85
philippensis, Petaurista, *Pteromys*, 85
Pholidota, 9, 101
picta, kerivoula, 30
picta, Viverra z., 53
pig, Wild, 67
pika, Curzon's, 100
pika, Forrest's, steppe, 99
pika, Himalayan, 100
pika, Royle's, or Himalayan, 99, 100
pileatus, Presbytis, *Semnopithecus*, 38
pipistrelle, Black gilded, 102
pipistrelle, Cadorna's, 28
pipistrelle, Indian, 27
pipistrelle, Javan, 26, 27
pipistrelle, Joffre's, 102
pipistrelle, Kelaart's, 26
pipistrelle, Least, 27
pipistrelle, Savi's, 27
Platanistidae, 63

platycephala, Crossopus, 14
***plicata, Tadarida*,** 31
plicatus, Vespertilio, 31
***pomona, Hipposideros*,** 22
***porcinus, Axis*,** *Cervus*, 70
porcupine, Asiatic brush-tailed, 97
porcupine, Crestless Himalayan, or Chinese, 96
porcupine, Indian crested, 97
Primates, 31, 102
primaevus, Cuon a., 43, 44
Prionailurus, 58
Proboscidea, 63
Prosimii, 32
***pruinosus, Rhizomys*,** 95
pruinosus, Ursus arctos, 44
Pteromyidae, 84, 102
Pteropodidae, 17
Pteropodinae, 17
***pusillus, Miniopterus*,** 29
***pusillus, Rhinolophus*,** 22
***pygerythrus, Callosciurus*,** *Sciurus*, 82
pygmaeoides, Crocidura *(Pachyura)*, 13

Q

***quadraticauda, Blarinella*,** 101

R

'rabbit', Assam, 98
***radulus, Soriculus*,** 12
ranjitsinhi, Cervus d., 69
rat, Bower's, 94
rat, Chestnut, 93
rat, Himalayan, 89
rat, House, Black, Roof, Ship, 89
rat, Indian bush, 90
rat", "Indian mole, 91
rat, Manipur, 94
rat, Millard's, or Large-toothed, 92
rat, Noisy, or Long-tailed giant, 94
rat, Smoke-bellied, 93
rat, White-bellied, 92
rattoides, Mus, 90
***rattus, Rattus*,** *Mus*, 89, 90
Ratufinae, 80
***remotus. Rattus*,** *Epimys*, 89
rhinoceros, Indian, or Greater one-horned, 65
rhinoceros, Sumatran, or Asian two-horned, 66
Rhinocerotidae, 65
Rhinolophidae, 21, 101
Rhinopomatidae, 101
Rhizomyinae, 95
Rodentia, 80, 102
Rodents, 80
***rouxii, Rhinolophus*,** 22
***roylei, Ochotona*,** 99
***roylei, Alticola*,** *Arvicola*, 95
roylii, Lagomys, 99
rubida, Capricornis, 78
rubricosa, Crocidura, 14
ruficaudatus, Lepus, 98
***rufigenis, Dremomys*,** *Sciurus*, 83

S

***saccolaimus, Taphozous*,** 20
sadiya, Lepus, 98
salvania, Porcula, 67
***salvanius, Sus*,** 67
Sambar, 69
***savii, Pipistrellus*,** *Vespertilio*, 27
Scandentia, 15
***schreibersii, Miniopterus*,** *Vespertilio*, 28
Sciuridae, 80
***scrofa, Sus*,** 67
Selenarctos, 45
Serotine, 101
serotinus, Eptesicus, 101
Serow, 77
serow, Burmese, or Red, 78
serow, Himalayan, 77
***setosus, Petinomys*,** 102
sheep, Blue, 79
sheep, Great Tibetan, 80
Shou, 70
shrew, Grey, 13
shrew, Himalayan water, 14
shrew, Hodgson's brown-toothed, 12
shrew, Horsfield's, 14
shrew, House or Grey musk, 12
shrew, Lesser stripe-backed, 11
shrew, Savi's pigmy, 13
shrew, Sichuan short-tailed, 101
shrew, Sikkim large-clawed, 11
shrew, Styan's water, 101
shrew, Szechuan burrowing, 14
***sibirica, Mustela*,** 48
sibiricus, Moschus, 69
***sicarius, Myotis*,** 24
sikkimensis, Pitymys, 102
sikkimensis, Rattus, 90
***siligorensis, Myotis*,** *Vespertilio*, 24
singhei, Petaurista n., 86
***sobrinus, Macroglossus*,** 19

soccatus, Sorex, 13
Soricidae, 11, 101
Soricinae, 11, 101
spasma, Megaderma, *Vespertilio,* 20
speciosa, Macaca, 38
spelaea, Eonycteris, *Macroglossus,* 19
sphinx, Cynopterus, *Vespertilio,* 18
squamipes, Anourosorex, 14
squirrel, Himalayan striped, 82
squirrel, Irrawaddy, or Himalayan hoary-bellied, 82
squirrel, Orange-bellied Himalayan, 83
squirrel, Pallas's, 81
squirrel, Perny's long-nosed, 83
squirrel, Red-cheeked, 83
stag, Sikkim, 70
strigidorsa, Mustela, 48
styani, Chimarrogale, 101
subbadius, Rhinolophus, 22
subcristata, Hystrix, 96
subflaviventris, Dremomys l., 83
Suidae, 67
sumatraensis, Capricornis, *Antilope,* 77
sumatrensis, Dicerorhinus, 66
Susu, 63
sylvaticus, Apodemus, *Mus,* 91

T

tahr, Himalayan, 102
Takin, 75, 78
Talpidae, 10, 101
Talpinae, 10, 101
taxicolor, Budorcas, 75
temminckii, Felis, 58
temminckii, Scotophilus, 25
tenaster, Niviventer, *Epimys,* 93
tenebricus, Presbytis, 39
teniotis, Tadarida, *Cephalotes,* 31
tenuis, Pipistrellus, *Vespertilio,* 27
thar, Antilope, 77
thibetana, Macaca, 35
thibetana, Ochotona, 99
thibetanus, Macacus, 35
thibetanus, Ursus, *Selenarctos,* 44, 45
thomasi, Rhinolophus, 101
tickelli, Hesperoptenus, *Nycticejus,* 28
tiger, Indian, or Bengal, 61
tigris, Panthera, *Felis,* 61
tistae, Rattus r., 89
Trachypithecus, 38
tralatitius, Vespertilio, 24
tree-shrew, Northern, 15
trifoliatus, Rhinolophus, 21
trivirgata, Arctogalidia, 55
trivirgatus, Paradoxurus, 55
tubinaris, Murina, *Harpiocephalus,* 29
Tupaiidae, 15
turkestanicus, Rattus, 90

U

uncia, Panthera, *Felis, Uncia,* 62
unicolor, Cervus, *C. axis,* 69
unicornis, Rhinoceros, 65
urbanus, Mus, 88
Uropsilinae, 101
Ursidae, 44
ursinus, Ursus, *Bradypus,* 46
urva, Herpestes, *Gulo,* 56

V

vaginalis, Cervus, 71
vampire, Greater or Indian false, 21
versurae, T. b., 16
Vespertilionidae, 24, 101
Vespertilioninae, 24, 101
vitticollis, Herpestes, 56
Viverridae, 52
Viverrinae, 52
viverrinus, Felis, 58
vole, Père David's, 95
vole, Royle's high mountain, 95
vole, Sikkim, 102
vulpes, Vulpes, *Canis,* 43

W

wallichi, Cervus, 70
weasel, Black-striped, 48
weasel, Siberian, 48
weasel, Yellow-bellied, 48
whitei, Budorcas t., 75
Wolf, 42
wolf, Tibetan, 42
wroughtoni, Dacnomys, 92

X

xanthipes,Trogopterus, 102

Y

yunanensis, Rhinolophus, 21

Z

zibetha, Viverra, 52